CHRISTMAS
RIBBONRY

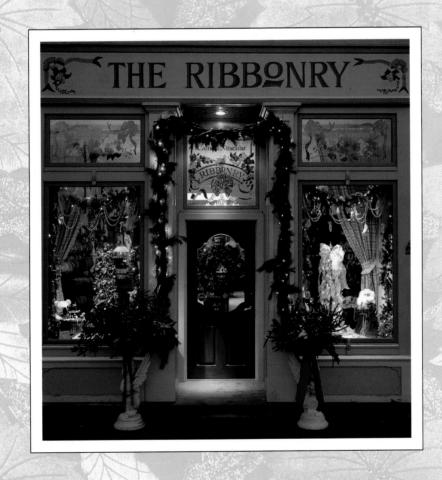

Camela Nitschke

CHRISTMAS
RIBBONRY

Edited by Marjon Schaefer

Pastimes™
An Imprint of Martingale & Company

Camela Nitschke
CHRISTMAS RIBBONRY

Copyright © 1998 by Landauer Corporation

This book was designed and produced by Landauer Books
A division of Landauer Corporation
12251 Maffitt Road, Cumming, Iowa 50061

President and Publisher: Jeramy Lanigan Landauer
Vice President: Becky Johnston
Editor-in-Chief: Marjon Schaefer
Art Director: Tracy DeVenney
Illustrator: Ann Weiss
Associate Editors: Marlene Hemberger Heuertz, Sarah Reid
Technical Editor: Tricia Coogan
Calligrapher: Cheryl O. Adams
Technical Assistant: Stewart Cott
Creative Assistant: Margaret Sindelar
Photographers: Craig Anderson, Amy Cooper, and Dennis Kennedy

Published by Martingale & Company
PO Box 118, Bothell, WA 98041-0118 USA

Library of Congress Cataloging-in-Publication Data
Nitschke, Camela, 1948-
    Christmas Ribbonry / Camela Nitschke; edited by Marjon Schaefer.
        p.   cm.
    Includes index.
    ISBN 1-56477-228-4 (softcover)
    1. Ribbon work. 2. Christmas decorations. I. Schaefer, Marjon.
  II. Title.
  TT850.5.N55 1998
746'.0476--dc21   98-16656
                                                         CIP

10 9 8 7 6 5 4 3 2 1

CONTENTS

Step inside Camela Nitschke's 1840s Federal-style home and discover a stunning collection of splendid ribbon creations to give as gifts or cherish for many years to come!

On long holiday evenings, retreat to the library to enjoy the sights, scents, and sounds of Christmas. The intimate setting shimmers with gold-ribbon accents on velvet stockings and a bright red poinsettia.

The music room provides a perfect setting to share time with loved ones. In seeking all that shimmers, Camela's choice of ornate ribbons, trims, and tassels is breathtaking and results in decorative accents that transcend the seasons.

FOREWORD

Christmas at our house always creates a flurry of activity. Family and friends naturally become the focus of this busy season, reminding me of how blessed I am to have loved ones to share and create happy memories with. The traditions handed down by my mother and grandmother are cherished legacies I share with my own children. I can remember my Grandmother placing pine boughs over the tops of our pictures and mirrors; then, with her guidance, the children helped decorate them with ribbons and small ornaments. This was something she had shared with her Grandmother as a child.

My mother recalls helping her Grandmother decorate for Christmas with garlands of red-and-green ribbons, festooned from corner to corner in a hallway of the old family home. She remembers winding nearly 100 yards of red plaid ribbon through pine boughs that decorated the hallway and staircase. Ornaments were packaged for reuse every year with great care. My mother and uncle both fondly remember watching wide-eyed as their Grandmother meticulously unwrapped a bright red bell that always hung from the center of the crisscrossed ribbon garland. Large stockings that hung from the mantels once held everything a Victorian child hoped to receive. My father recalls the traditional oranges and nuts and neatly packed small gifts, like boxes of chocolate and yo-yo's and hockey pucks, and for the girls, lengths of ribbon. In our home, this tradition is an important one. In place of Grandfather's old socks, woven-ribbon stockings are hung every year in our eldest daughter's bedroom and filled with much the same traditional contents, with the addition of a new ribbon ornament every year. Checking out the stockings and snacking on the fruit and candies keeps the children occupied while my husband and I prepare with camera in hand for their rapid descent down the staircase, which must happen en masse.

I enjoy the days of preparation that go into decorating for holiday parties. Choosing a color theme to complement my home and creating a festive mood excites me. A beautiful woven jacquard or equally beautiful metallic stripe ribbon inspires baskets full of rich ribbon ornaments. I love to invent contemporary applications for ribbon decorations. In fact, most ornaments in this book have a history in the millinery trade and were once the main features on ladies' hats. Too large and cumbersome for contemporary use on hats, they're perfect as ornaments. The folded-ribbon cocardes and galettes are truly heirlooms for future generations. Practice makes perfect, and you'll find that practicing with less expensive ribbons is not only fun but also helps you prepare for more challenging versions of these simple ornaments.

Ornaments made from a jacquard ribbon that won't be around long make the ideal gift. After all, ornaments don't only pertain to Christmas. A gift of a ribbon ornament is a memory from the past, an heirloom to be treasured long after the ribbon has disappeared.

9

WELCOME

Softly falling snow in the early December dusk poetically envelopes Camela Nitschke's 1840s Federal-style home in Perrysburg, Ohio. Step inside and discover how Camela embraces the holiday season with a stunning collection of splendid ribbon creations to give as gifts or cherish for many years to come!

WELCOME

In a season of glad tidings and good wishes, let everyone who enters experience the joy of hearth and home with a rich medley of festive holiday trims and inspirations.

Adornment begins in the entrance hall, where an exuberant garland of greenery festoons the staircase banister in a grand manner. Crimson ribbon poinsettias with sparkling gold centers punctuate each deep swag, which in turn glows with the addition of five-petal flower clusters in colors chosen to enhance the country flowers on the wallpaper. Artistry in bloom, each blossom becomes almost real in the expert hands of Camela.

The splendor reaches a crescendo with a brass chandelier trimmed in Yuletide grandeur with a large kissing ball fashioned of evergreen and an abundance of ribbon loops.

WELCOME

There's joy as well as history in creating beautiful ribbon flowers, especially poinsettias resplendent in full bloom at Christmas.

Viewed as a lowly weed the people of Mexico call "Flower of the Holy Night," the plant with deep green leaves and crimson blooms (really the top leaves!) was brought to the United States in 1825 by Joel Roberts Poinsett, America's first ambassador to Mexico. When Poinsett returned to his native Charleston, South Carolina, with this exotic blooming plant, it was officially named poinsettia.

Now firmly established as a symbol of the season, the poinsettia spreads Christmas cheer in colors ranging from deep crimson to pale pink, snowy white, and even variegated varieties.

It is this remarkable color versatility that makes the poinsettia ideal for any Christmas decorating scheme—from rustic country to opulent Gilded-Age.

Dress your home for the holidays with a myriad of these dazzling blooms in their ribbon-wrought versions, then scatter them on everything, from eager-to-please packages to a rich and colorful staircase swag and crisp window wreath as shown opposite.

The technique for handcrafting poinsettias in three different sizes is outlined in the back of the book; you'll be amazed to discover how easy it is to make them in multiples to create a tapestry of Christmas color that gladdens the heart and holiday home.

KISSING BALL

MATERIALS

- 3 yards of 1"-wide green or red pleated ribbon
- 5 yards of 2½"-wide plaid ribbon
- 4 yards of 1"-wide gold metallic ribbon to make six M bows (see page 105)
- 2 yards of 2½"-wide gold metallic wire-edge ribbon
- 6" Styrofoam ball
- Package of wooden picks with florist's wire attached
- Fresh boxwood
- Paddle wire

INSTRUCTIONS

1. Wrap paddle wire vertically around ball several times so the ball ends up looking like a peeled orange. At the top of the ball, where the wires intersect, create a 1" to 2" hanger by looping the wire several times around the intersection.

2. Cut 2"- to 3"-long sprigs of boxwood. Remove the leaves from the bottom inch of each sprig; gently force this end into the ball. Cover the ball with boxwood.

3. Cut twenty 6" pieces of plaid ribbon and ten 6" pieces of green or red pleated ribbon. Referring to the illustration, below, shape each piece into a loop and wire the ends to the wooden pick. Cut six 24" pieces of 1" gold metallic ribbon and, referring to the instructions on page 105, make six M bows. Wire the bows to picks.

4. Insert the picks into the ball, making sure the loops and bows are evenly arranged. Keep them mainly on the sides of the ball, leaving room at the bottom and the top.

5. Using the remaining ribbons, create loops, each with one or two long tails attached; wire to the wooden picks.

6. Insert the picks into the bottom and top of the ball, making sure the longer tails are on the bottom. When you're pleased with the arrangement, trim the ends of the tails into an inverted V shape.

7. Attach a length of strong monofilament or wire to the hanging loop. Hang the ball from a light fixture, ceiling grid, or as desired.

CHRISTMAS GARLAND

MATERIALS

- Evergreen roping

- Boxwood or other evergreen with leaves rather than needles

- Flower clusters (see page 18)

- 2½ yards of 1¾"-wide red wire-edge ribbon for each large poinsettia (see page 112)

- 2 yards of ½"-wide gold metallic braid

- Ball of twine or string

- Florist's wire

INSTRUCTIONS

1. Determine the length of the roping as follows: Measure the length of the staircase railing. For every 3 feet of railing, figure 4½ feet of roping. Calculate the length, then add the height of the newel post to the total. Purchase or create the roping.

2. Drape the roping in place, wrapping it around the railing at 3-foot intervals and swagging 4½ feet of roping for every 3 feet of railing. To wrap the roping around the railing, insert it between two spindles, then wrap it over the railing to the front to start the next swag. Neatly secure the roping with twine wherever it wraps around the railing.

3. Make as many poinsettias as you have high points in the roping, including the top of the newel post. Cut two 6" pieces of florist's wire for each poinsettia. Twist the wires so they intertwine. Using a few overhand stitches, sew the center of the wires to the back of the poinsettia in the center of the buckram; secure a large poinsettia to each high point. If it looks like the wire may scratch the railing, use a short length of twine or string instead. You will not get as nice a tie as with wire, but it will protect your railing.

4. Make two flower clusters for each swagged section of roping. If desired, make a flower cluster for that portion of the roping that hangs alongside the newel post. Attach each cluster with florist's wire. Randomly add the boxwood or other evergreen.

FLOWER CLUSTER

MATERIALS

- 23½" each of four 1¼"- to 2"-wide assorted ribbons to make four five-petal flowers (see page 102)

- 8" of 2"-wide gold metallic-mesh ribbon to make four flower centers (see page 103)

- 7" each of seven 1"-wide assorted green and gold wire-edge ribbons to make seven leaves (see page 104)

- 12" of 1"-wide red and/or green gold-edge organdy ribbon to make three pods (see page 121)

- 27" of 2"-wide gold wire-edge metallic-mesh ribbon

- 3" x 6" piece of buckram

- Standard sewing supplies

INSTRUCTIONS

1. Referring to the pages mentioned in the materials list, make four five-petal flowers, four flower centers, seven assorted leaves, and three pods.

2. To make the three-loop flourish at the end of the cluster, cut one 10", one 9", and one 8" length of gold metallic ribbon. Individually, fold each length in half, form a small pleat at each end, and secure the pleated ends together with a few small stitches. Referring to the illustration, below, layer the loops so the ends all match up, placing the largest loop on the bottom and the smallest loop at the top. Sew the three loops together at the cut ends. Attach the end of the loop frill to the center of a 3" end of the buckram.

3. Referring to the photgraph, left, position the leaves, flowers, and pods on the buckram, moving them around until you are pleased with the arrangement. Using neutral or matching threads, sew the components in place, beginning with the leaves, then the pods, and finally, the flowers. Trim away the excess buckram around the outer edges only, leaving a solid center foundation.

4. The cluster is now ready to be used for a variety of projects. To be able to secure it to a garland, work as follows: Cut six 10" pieces of florist's wire. Make two bundles of three wires each and twist each bundle so the wires intertwine. Using a few overhand stitches, sew the center of each bundle to the back of the cluster, about one-third and two-thirds down the center of the buckram.

Wreath

Materials

- 18" pine wreath

- 1½ yards each of ¼"- and ½"-wide gold-mesh flat braid

- 6 yards of 1½"-wide white with gold metallic wire-edge ribbon to make three medium poinsettias (see pages 112–113)

- 7½ yards of ⅝"-wide red metallic wire-edge ribbon to make five small poinsettias (see pages 112–113)

- Standard sewing supplies

- Florist's wire

Instructions

1. Cut each length of gold-mesh braid into three equal lengths. Tie an overhand knot about 2½" from both ends of each length, then tie an overhand knot in the center of each length. Referring to the illustration, right, fold the ribbons so the knots are all at one end, and the ribbon tails and the folds on the other end. Secure the tails and folds with a few stitches.

2. Prepare the gold and red poinsettias according to the poinsettia instructions on pages 112–113.

3. If desired, attach the ends of some of the gold ribbon loops to the buckram bases of a few poinsettias. Wrap florist's wire around the ends of the remaining loops so they can be wired into the wreath.

4. Cut two 6" pieces of florist's wire for each poinsettia. Twist the wires so they intertwine. Using a few overhand stitches, sew the center of the wires to the back of the poinsettia in the center of the buckram.

5. Wire the poinsettias and the loops to the wreath in a crescent shape, leaving the remaining portion of the wreath just plain green.

READ & RELAX

swirl decorative flourish

*Long winter evenings provide
the perfect excuse for a retreat
to the library to enjoy the
solitude so necessary for finding
the quiet center of life.
In this intimate setting, the
scents of pine, leather, and
fresh-brewed tea blend
beautifully with the sights of
rich ribbons and trims of special
holiday creations—a bright red
poinsettia to perk up a package
and a gorgeous turbine rose with
an antique-gold button center,
lavished with shimmering
ribbon streamers.*

21

READ & RELAX

Oh, it's so easy to while away the hours while cocooned in the close confines of a pine-paneled library. Nestled in a cozy and cushy leather chair with a good classic book on your lap and warmed by the heat of a brightly blazing fire, you slowly drift off into a contemplative state of peace and contentment that allows the mind to become creative and fruitful.

Banded with antique and imported ribbons, the stockings are hung from the mantel with care—of course, it's best to remove the stockings before the fire turns into a roaring blaze! The mantel itself is splendidly dressed in a tassel-trimmed shawl of ribbon-striped velvet scallops that inherit their shape from the antique needlepoint-and-beaded candle shields made by Camela's great-great-grandmother.

A turbine rose with multiple ribbon streamers tops off the fireplace splendor and serves as an elegant accent for the steel engraving framed in fresh holiday greenery. The Scottish engraving was a favorite hunt picture of Camela's great-great-grandfather James Cummings, who came from Perthshire, Scotland.

Punctuated by a few additional treasures, such as an heirloom pewter teapot and a doll dressed in fantasy fashions of a faraway country, the room exudes an elegant old-world ambience. A lampshade trimmed for the holidays and the comforts of a spectacular ribbon-striped pillow and afghan add finishing touches to this inviting and restful retreat.

A private place for quiet reflection, relaxation, and reading is greatly enhanced by the soft amber glow of candlelight or the warm welcoming rays gently streaming from a shaded lamp. Here, transform an ordinary white shade into an elegant holiday statement with the simple addition of a triple-box-pleated ribbon along the bottom edge. A narrow velvet ribbon holds a simple band of pleated ribbon along the top edge, and a stunning tasseled medallion ties it all together.

A favorite chair invites you to delve into a book or to just
lie back and listen to Christmas classics while snuggled
under a gentle-to-the-touch wool afghan with matching
pillow. Because the ribbon edges are finished, the need for
seams is eliminated and the embellishments work up quickly
from varying lengths and widths of ribbons, needing only
mitered corners for a graphic effect with great impact.

Turbine Trim

Materials

- 3 yards of 3½"-wide red cut-velvet and satin ribbon to make one turbine rose (see page 120)

- 3⅓ yards of ½"-wide gold lace

- 1¾" button with center decoration

- 23½" of 3"-wide green iridescent organdy ribbon to make one five-petal flower (see page 102)

- 1½ yards of 3½"-wide red cut-velvet and satin ribbon

- 2 yards of 1"-wide green pleated ribbon

- 2 yards of 1½"-wide gold wire-edge ribbon

- Florist's wire

- Standard sewing supplies

Instructions

1. Cut off a 12" length of gold lace and set aside. Sew the remaining 3 yards of gold lace to the bottom edge of the 3-yard length of cut-velvet and satin ribbon. Refer to page 120 to make one turbine rose.

2. Fold the green iridescent ribbon lengthwise so one long edge of the ribbon is ⅜" higher than the other. Referring to the instructions on page 102, make a five-petal flower, measuring off 4½" spaces for each petal.

3. Tack the five-petal flower to the center of the turbine rose. Gather the remaining 12" of gold lace and sew it around the back edge of the button. Sew the button to the center of the turbine rose.

4. To make the streamers, cut the 1½ yards of red-velvet and satin ribbon in half; tack the ribbons together at one end, offsetting the ends somewhat so the streamers angle out. Sew the turbine rose atop the tacked end of the streamers.

5. Using the remaining ribbons, create loops with long streamers attached. Bundle the loops and streamers; when you're pleased with the arrangement, tack them together at the top. Trim the ends of the streamers into an inverted V shape.

6. Secure the loop arrangement to the red velvet and satin streamers, underneath the petals of the turbine rose.

7. The turbine trim is now ready to be used in a variety of ways. To be able to secure it to a garland or nail, work as follows: Cut two 6" pieces of florist's wire. Twist the wires so they intertwine. Using a few overhand stitches, sew the center of the wires to the back of the rose, where the velvet and satin streamers are tacked together.

LAMPSHADE TRIM

MATERIALS

- 1⅛"-wide plaid taffeta ribbon to make triple-pleated ribbon edging (see page 111)

- ¼"-wide gold cord

- ⅝"-wide green pleated ribbon

- 10" of 1⅛"-wide plaid taffeta ribbon

- ⅜"-wide cranberry double-sided velvet ribbon

- 3" brass button

- Two 2" gold tassels

- 3" square of buckram

- Standard sewing supplies

- Hot-glue gun and glue sticks

INSTRUCTIONS

1. Starting and ending at the center back of the shade and using dots of hot glue on the bottom edge of the back of the ribbon, apply ⅝" green pleated ribbon along the top edge of the lampshade so the top edge of the ribbon extends ⅛" above the shade's edge. Cover the lower edge of the pleated ribbon with ⅜" velvet ribbon by applying dots of hot glue to the back of the velvet ribbon.

2. Cut 12" of velvet ribbon and fold in half, forming an upside-down V. Glue the fold to the center front of the lampshade, just underneath the ribbon trim.

3. Sew the short edges of the 10" length of plaid ribbon together to form a circle. Sew gathering stitches along one edge of the circle. Draw up the gathering thread until a ¼" opening remains in the center. Secure the gathering thread. Sew the circle to the center of the buckram.

4. Using 3" of the green pleated ribbon, make a similar circle; however, there is no need to gather the ribbon since it's already pleated. Sew the green circle to the center of the buckram, through the center of the plaid circle. Sew the button to the center. Trim the buckram.

5. Glue this decoration to the center front of the lampshade, on the bottom edge of the ribbon trim. Loop the gold tassels over the button.

6. Referring to the instructions on page 111, make enough triple-pleated edging to go around the bottom edge of the lampshade. Starting and ending at the center back of the shade and using dots of hot glue on the back of the ribbon, apply the triple-pleated plaid ribbon trim along the bottom edge of the lampshade so the bottom edge of the ribbon extends ¼" below the shade's edge. Starting and ending at the center back of the shade, string ¼" gold cord through the top layer of the triple-pleated trim.

PILLOW

MATERIALS

- 1 yard of blue velvet fabric
- 2½" yards of metallic cording
- 28" of 1¾"-wide embroidered ribbon
- 1½ yards of ⅞"-wide gold ribbon
- 1⅛ yards of 1⅛"-wide gold embroidered ribbon
- 2⅛ yards of 1½"-wide taffeta ribbon
- Polyester fiberfill
- Sewing machine
- Standard sewing supplies

INSTRUCTIONS

1. From blue velvet, cut two 19" x 22" pieces. Mark a 1¾" x 4¼" rectangle in the center of one velvet panel. Set the second panel aside.

2. Beginning along one 4¼" edge, pin the 1¾" ribbon around the marked rectangle, mitering the corners. Make sure the corners are crisp 90-degree angles.

Overlap the ends and turn under the visible end ½". Sew the ribbon in place with matching thread. Pin the ⅞" gold ribbon around the first ribbon row, again making sure the mitered corners are crisp angles; sew in place. Next, sew the 1⅛" and the 1½" ribbons in place.

3. Using a ½" seam allowance, pin the metallic cording all around the right-side edges of the decorated velvet panel. Sew in place on the stitching line of the cording.

4. Place the velvet pieces with right sides together and sew all around three edges and four corners, leaving an opening for the pillow stuffing.

5. To make the three-loop flourish at the corner of the rectangle, cut one 8", one 7", and one 5" length of ⅞"-wide gold metallic ribbon. Individually, fold each length in half, form a small pleat at each end, and secure the pleated ends together with a few small stitches. Referring to the illustration, below, layer the loops so the ends all match up, placing the largest loop on the bottom and the smallest loop at the top. Sew the three loops together at the cut ends. Cut one 2" length of gold ribbon and wrap around the end of the flourish; sew in back. Attach the end of the flourish to one of the gold-ribbon corners on the front of the pillow.

6. Stuff the pillow with fiberfill.

BLANKET

MATERIALS

- 51" x 63" piece of wool plaid blanket fabric
- 7 yards of 1⅝"-wide blue taffeta ribbon
- 7 yards of ¾"-wide green taffeta ribbon
- 1 yard of 1½"-wide embroidered ribbon
- 1 yard of 1⅝"-wide taffeta ribbon
- 1 yard of 1½"-wide embroidered ribbon
- 1 yard of 1⅛"-wide blue taffeta ribbon
- 1 yard of ⅞"-wide gold ribbon
- 1 yard of 1⅛"-wide plaid taffeta ribbon
- Sewing machine
- Standard sewing supplies

INSTRUCTIONS

1. Zigzag the edges of the wool plaid with matching thread. Turn a ½" hem to the right side and stitch in place.

2. Set aside the first two ribbons on the materials list. Sew the remaining six ribbons together in the order that they appear on the materials list, topstitching one onto just the edge of the next one, and so forth.

3. Pin-mark the edges of the ribbon fabric where shown with dots in the illustration, below. Cut the fabric where indicated with solid lines. Referring to X and Y labels, match up the pieces in pairs. Join the pairs at the angle-

cut A-B edges; two pairs with the embroidered ribbon in the outside corner, and two pairs with the embroidered ribbon along the inside edges. Sew the pieces together, creating four corner blocks with faux mitered corners. Press the seam allowances open.

4. Pin the blocks in the corners of the blanket, with the inside corner of the block closest to the corner of the blanket and leaving a 2" space between the block and the blanket edges.

5. Sew the blocks in place, sewing on each previous stitching line if preferred.

6. Beginning along one 63" edge, pin the 1⅝" blue taffeta ribbon all around the blanket, covering the hem and mitering the corners. Make sure the corners are at crisp 90-degree angles. Topstitch the ribbon in place with matching thread. Pin the ¾" green taffeta ribbon inside the first ribbon row, again making sure the corners form crisp angles. This round should cover the outer edges of the corner blocks. Topstitch in place with matching thread.

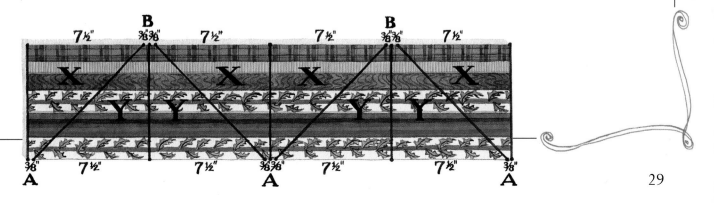

Velvet Stockings

Materials

- ¾ yard of green velvet for one stocking

- ½ yard each of any medium-weight green fancy fabric and muslin for foundation of ribbon

- Several coordinating ribbons, trims, cords, and flat lace pieces in a variety of widths

- ¾ yard of green taffeta to line stocking

- Matching threads

- 2½"-wide green pleated organdy ribbon

- 4" tassel

- Sewing machine

- Standard sewing supplies

Instructions

1. For a full-size stocking pattern, increase the pattern, right, on a photocopy machine until the squares on the grid equal 1". Trace the stocking top and toe patterns from your full-size pattern.

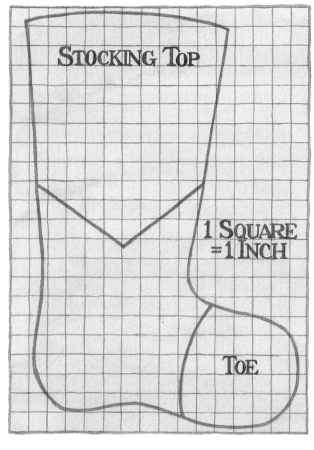

STOCKING TOP

1 SQUARE = 1 INCH

TOE

2. For one stocking, cut two stocking pieces each from green velvet and green taffeta, reversing the direction of one piece for each fabric. Cut one stocking top and one toe each from green fancy fabric and from muslin.

3. Arrange an assortment of ribbons and lace either horizontally or vertically across the front of the green stocking top and toe pieces, letting the fabric show through in some places so it becomes part of design. To add to your design, gather both edges of some ribbon pieces before placing them onto the foundation, see below; then cover the stitching with neighboring ribbons, cording, or narrow trim. Knife-pleat some ribbons, following the technique described on page 110. When you are pleased with the arrangement, topstitch the ribbons in place.

4. With right sides together and ½" seam allowances, sew a matching muslin piece to the pointed end of the stocking top and to the inside curve of the toe piece, leaving any edges that will be caught in the seams of the stocking unstitched. Turn the muslin to the back of the foundation fabric. If desired, hand-stitch cording along these seams. With all raw edges matching, baste both of the ribbon-embellished pieces right side up on the right side of one velvet stocking piece.

5. With right sides together and a ½" seam allowance, sew the front stocking to the back velvet stocking, leaving the top edge open. Clip curves and turn right side out.

6. With right sides together and a ½" seam allowance, sew the front lining to the back lining, leaving the top straight edge open.

7. With wrong sides together, place the lining inside the velvet stocking. Turn in the top edge of the stocking and hand-sew it closed.

8. Referring to the instructions for making serpentine trim, below, gather enough 2½"-wide pleated organdy ribbon to fit across the top of the stocking in the front only. Hand-sew the ribbon across the top edge of the stocking.

9. Hand-sew a tassel to the point of the embellished stocking top.

10. Fold a short length of narrow ribbon or cord in half and sew to the top back corner of the stocking for a hanging loop.

SERPENTINE TRIM

1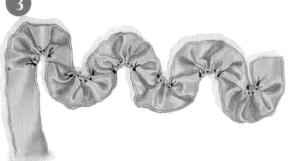

2

3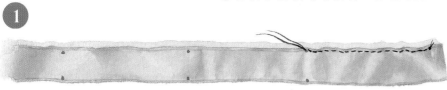

1. Use tailor's chalk to mark evenly spaced intervals across both selvedges of the ribbon. To determine the length of each interval, multiply the ribbon width by 3.5. Examples: 3.5 x 1" ribbon is 3.5" or 3½" intervals; 3.5 x 1.5" ribbon = 5.25" or 5¼" intervals.

2. Using doubled thread, sew running stitches across the top selvedge between the first and second marks. Pull the thread tight to gather the ribbon; knot and clip the thread in back. Sew running stitches across the bottom selvedge between the second and third marks. Pull the thread tight to gather the ribbon; knot and clip the thread. Continue to stitch across the ribbon in the same way, remembering to alternate the edges.

3. To calculate the length of ribbon needed, use the following formula: (3.5 x ribbon width) x finished length. Example: For a 24" trim using 1½"-wide ribbon, you will need (3.5 x 1.5") x 24" = 126" or 3½ yards. (Allow an additional ½" at each end for turning under.)

DO YOU
HEAR WHAT
I HEAR?

A rhapsody in blue, the music room is
a symphony of jeweled treasures
to share with family and friends. In seeking all
that shimmers, Camela's choice of ornate
ribbons, trims, and tassels is breathtaking
in its simple magnificence.
Here and on the following pages
you'll find enticing ribbon-embellished
projects to gild your holiday home or
to give to a treasured friend.

Delicate organdy ornaments stand out in stark contrast to the white-painted birch branches from which they hang, providing a splendid enhancement of the view from the music room window. The pastel-hued galettes are easy and quick to make in multiples, while ordinary silver glass balls go from ho-hum to heavenly in minutes when topped with jaunty, ethereal M bows. A larger galette, left, makes quite a statement as a package topper or tree ornament. Additional lace, an antique button, and a few tassels add panache.

If the idea of Christmas ribbonry intrigues you, you'll find enchantments galore in this treasure trove of ribbon gifts and trims. Finely crafted and wrapped with love, this collection of unique designs includes an elegant ribbon-woven and tasseled evening bag, ribbon flowers for packages, and one-of-a-kind Christmas stockings that range in size from large, for filling with secret surprises, to very small, for filling in the small open spaces between the Christmas tree branches.

W

With a rich frosting of delicate roses, holly and evergreens grace the mantel in the music room, lending a special high note of yuletide cheer.

For this ruffled ribbon confection, Camela chose yards of ribbon in soft shades of pink, blue, and gold to match the softly understated decor of the music room, which is filled with family antiques, quaint collectibles, and framed photos of loved ones. Cabochon roses and Renoir roses, velvet picot-edge and shiny gold ribbon loops, and seven-petal flowers combine into a color concerto that delights the senses.

The presence of a cherished 1920s Starr piano—bought at an auction at the local high school, where it accompanied many a Christmas pageant—defines the gentle space with the promise of Christmas carols: traditional melodies of old to be sung in harmony when dusk is nigh and the glow of candlelight casts a magic spell into the farthest reaches of the room.

And even when the magic of Christmas has become but a lingering memory, the garland swag of ribbon roses in all its pastel glory still complements the gracious decor the remaining seasons of the year.

Package Ornament

Materials

- 2 yards of 1"-wide gold metallic mesh ribbon to make one twisted étoile (see page 101)

- 12" of 1"-wide gold metallic lace to make one ruffled center

- 14" of 1"-wide gold metallic mesh ribbon to make one button center (see page 86)

- 6" of gold cord for hanger (optional)

Instructions

1. Following the instructions on page 101, make a twisted étoile from gold metallic mesh ribbon.

2. Sew the short edges of the gold metallic lace together to form a circle. Sew gathering stitches along one edge of the circle. Draw up the gathering thread until a ½" opening is left in the center. Secure the gathering thread. Tack the gathered ribbon to the center of the twisted étoile.

3. Following the instructions on pages 86–87, make a button center from gold metallic mesh ribbon. Tack the button center to the center of the twisted étoile.

4. To make a hanging ornament, bring the ends of the gold cord together and sew to the back of one petal.

Galette Ornaments

Materials

- 1½ yards of 1"-wide pink, white, or blue iridescent organdy ribbon to make one small galette (see page 98)

- 8" of ½"-wide iridescent organdy ribbon to make one small M bow (see page 105)

- 3½ yards of 2¾"-wide ribbon to make one large galette (see page 98)

- 1 yard of 3"-wide pink taffeta ribbon to make one large M bow (see page 105)

- Several lengths of cord or narrow ribbon for hanging

- 3" gold button for the large galette

- Two 3" purchased tassels for the large galette

Instructions

1. Refer to the instructions on page 98 to make the small or large galette.

2. Refer to the instructions on page 105 to make the M bows.

3. Enhance the ornaments as desired.

4. Bring together the ends of the cord and sew to the back of the ornament.

GARLAND

MATERIALS

- Buckram

- Cloth-covered bridal wire

- 1 yard of 1¾"-wide wire-edge taffeta, grosgrain, or organdy ribbon for each one of 60 roses (see pages 88–89) and 4" for each one of 18 rosebuds

- 7 yards of 1"-wide green wire-edge taffeta ribbon for 36 leaves (see page 104)

- 48" of 1⅛"-wide velvet ribbon for eight loops

- 2 yards of 2½"-wide silver or gold ribbon braid for 12 loops

- 10 yards of ⅞"-wide white organdy ribbon for 12 seven-petal flowers (see page 102)

- One bunch of stamens

- Matching threads; four ¾" curtain rings

- Newsprint or pattern paper, ruler, and pencil

- Hot-glue gun and glue sticks

- Sewing machine; standard sewing supplies

INSTRUCTIONS

1. The following requirements are for a garland measuring 66" long. For a longer or shorter garland, change the requirements. Tape together a 66" length of newsprint or pattern paper and fold into thirds. Draw lines across paper as indicated by the gray lines in the illustration, top right, then draw one section of the garland as indicated by the green lines. Cut out the garland pattern; unfold the paper. Use the pattern to cut five layers of buckram.

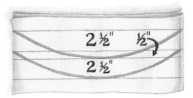

2. Stack the layers of cut buckram and sew together every ½" for a sturdy foundation. Zigzag-stitch a length of bridal wire along the center and top edge of foundation.

3. Make 20 cabochon roses for each section of the garland, varying the colors and types of ribbon used and the length of each ribbon. (If you've changed the length of the garland, adjust the number of pieces to fit.) Make four Renoir roses—one for each point of the garland.

4. Using 4" of 1¾" wire-edge ribbon for each rosebud, make six buds for each section of garland, following the first five steps for making a cabochon rose.

5. Using 30" of organdy ribbon for each seven-petal flower, make three flowers for each section of garland. Glue several stamens to the center of each flower.

6. Using 7" of green 1" wire-edge taffeta for the first leaf, make 12 leaves for each section of the garland. Vary them by using different lengths.

7. Glue the roses and seven-petal flowers to the buckram foundation. Fill in with rosebuds and leaves. Finally, cut ribbon braid and velvet ribbon into 6" lengths and fold each in half to make a loop. Glue the loops among the flowers and leaves.

8. Hand-sew a ¾" curtain ring to the back of each point of the garland, with its top edge matching the top edge of the buckram.

WOVEN PURSE

MATERIALS

- Iron-on interfacing
- Large piece of foamcore board
- Several yards of coordinating ribbons in a variety of widths and colors to make the woven-ribbon fabric (see page 122)
- Fabric that coordinates with ribbons for purse lining
- Matching thread
- 1 yard of satin cording
- One large snap
- Pencil and ruler
- Sewing machine
- Standard sewing supplies

INSTRUCTIONS

Note: The fabric for the purse is created by cross-weaving a variety of ribbons following the technique described on page 122. The weaving is done on a base of iron-on interfacing. When the weaving is completed, the ribbons are secured to the iron-on interfacing so they cannot shift.

1. Draw a 10½" x 16" rectangle onto both sides of the iron-on interfacing. Mark the fold lines on both sides as shown below, and a 45-degree angle on the adhesive side only. Pin the corners of the interfacing piece, adhesive side up, to the foamcore board.

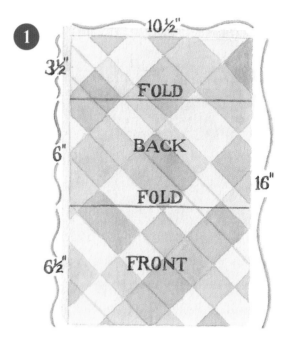

Referring to instructions for ribbon weaving on page 122, cover the interfacing pattern with woven ribbons. Fuse the ribbons in place, then stitch around the entire rectangle, stitching just inside the pattern lines. Cut out the rectangle on the drawn pattern lines.

2. Fold the bottom third of the purse up along the marked fold line. Fold and press a ½" seam allowance along the top edge of the folded section. Unfold the just-pressed seam allowance slightly so as not to catch it in the side seams. Using ½" seam allowances, stitch the side seams as shown, below, and catching the ends of the cording in the top of the seams at A and B at the same time.

3. Measure and cut out a same-size lining piece. With right sides together, fold the bottom third up and press in a ½" seam allowance from A to B. Stitch the side seams as shown below, but widen the seam allowances gradually from ½ inch at A and B to ¾" as you get closer to the bottom fold.

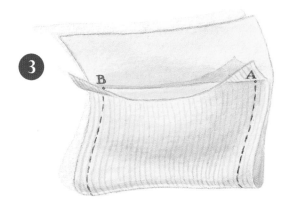

4. Place the lining panel on top of the woven-ribbon panel with right sides together, and all edges and points A and B matching. Using ½" seam allowances, sew the the flaps of both panels together, sewing from A to the top left corner, then across the top edge, then from the top right corner down to B as shown below. Trim the corners and seam allowances.

5. Turn the flap and the woven-ribbon purse pocket right side out. Do not turn the lining purse pocket right side out. Slip the lining pocket inside the woven-ribbon pocket. Neatly handsew the pressed edges together. Fold the flap over the purse front and determine the snap placement. Attach the snaps. Use leftover ribbon to decorate the front of the purse with a bow or flower as desired.

Woven Stocking

Materials

- Stocking pattern (you can use the pattern on page 30 or purchase the pattern of your choice)

- Iron-on interfacing

- Large piece of foamcore board

- Several yards of coordinating ribbons and flat lace in a variety of widths to make the woven-ribbon fabric (see page 122)

- Fabric that coordinates with ribbons for back of stocking and for lining

- Matching thread

- Purchased gold tassel and short length of matching gold cord

- 1½"-wide ribbon to make the triple box-pleated trim (see page 111)

- Pencil

- Sewing machine

- Standard sewing supplies

Instructions

Note: The fabric for the stocking is created by cross-weaving a variety of ribbons following the technique described on page 122. The weaving is done on a base of iron-on interfacing. When the weaving is completed, the ribbons are secured to the iron-on interfacing so they cannot shift.

1. Draw a stocking shape onto both sides of a piece of iron-on interfacing. You can draw the shape freehand, or trace a purchased stocking or stocking pattern. Remember to include a seam allowance. Pin the corners of the interfacing piece, adhesive side up, to the foamcore board.

2. Referring to the instructions for ribbon weaving on page 122, cover the interfacing pattern with woven ribbons. If desired, weave narrower ribbons and flat lace on top of the wider ribbons. Fuse the ribbons in place. Place the ribbon fabric interfacing side up so the pattern lines are visible, and stitch just inside the pattern lines. Cut out the stocking on the pattern lines.

3. Use the woven-ribbon stocking as a pattern to cut out the back of stocking and two lining pieces from any coordinating fabric.

4. Sew the woven-ribbon stocking to the back stocking, with right sides together and leaving the top edge open. Clip the curves. Turn the stocking right side out; press.

5. With right sides together and leaving the top edge open, sew the front lining stocking to the back lining stocking. With wrong sides together, place the lining stocking inside the ribbon stocking. Turn in the top edges and hand-sew closed, inserting the ends of a short length of cord for a hanging loop and the ends of a gold tassel before sewing the top edge closed at the back seam.

6. Referring to the instructions for making a triple box pleat with a ½" gauge on page 111, pleat enough 1½"-wide ribbon to fit across the top edge of the stocking front. Hand-sew the pleated trim in place.

WOVEN MINI STOCKINGS

MATERIALS

- Stocking pattern
- Iron-on interfacing
- Foamcore board
- Several yards of coordinating ribbons and flat lace in a variety of widths to make the woven-ribbon fabric (see page 122)
- Short length of gold metallic fringe
- 3" of narrow gold braid or cord for hanging loop
- Fabric that coordinates with ribbons for back of stocking
- Matching thread
- Polyester stuffing
- Pencil
- Sewing machine
- Standard sewing supplies

INSTRUCTIONS

Note: The fabric for the stocking ornaments is created by cross-weaving a variety of ribbons following the technique described on page 122. The weaving is done on a base of iron-on interfacing. When the weaving is completed, the ribbons are secured to the iron-on interfacing so they cannot shift.

1. Draw a small stocking shape onto both sides of the iron-on interfacing. Pin the corners of the interfacing piece, adhesive side up, to the foamcore board.

2. Referring to the instructions for ribbon weaving on page 122, cover the interfacing pattern with woven ribbons. For an interesting effect, weave narrower ribbons and flat lace ribbons on top of the wider ribbons. Fuse the ribbons in place. Place the ribbon fabric interfacing side up so the pattern lines are visible, and stitch just inside the pattern lines. Cut out the stocking on the pattern lines.

3. With right sides up, pin a length of gold metallic fringe across the top edge of the ribbon stocking.

4. Reverse the stocking pattern and cut out the back of the stocking from a coordinating fabric.

5. With right sides together, sew the two stocking pieces together, leaving the straight top edge open. Clip the curves, turn the stocking right side out, and insert stuffing. Turn in the raw edges at the top, and neatly hand-sew the top closed.

6. Fold a short length of narrow braid or cord in half and sew to the back top corner for a hanging loop. Attach a small bow below the hanging loop.

PEACEFUL
RETREAT

*E*veryone needs a nook for relaxation and
quiet reflection, especially during the hectic
holiday season. For Camela Nitschke, an
enclosed porch off the kitchen is the perfect
place to spend a few precious moments in the
soft glow of candlelight, surrounded by her
favorite Christmas collectibles, flowers, and
quilts. In this serene setting, Camela takes
pleasure in filling ribbon-trimmed moiré
stockings with small wrapped gifts for the
children to discover later.

PEACEFUL RETREAT

One of the finest pleasures of the porch is the opportunity for friends and family to gather 'round a primitive pine farm table in a relaxed setting of mismatched chairs. Camela finds this casual mix a delightful challenge to blend color, texture, and pattern in the table runner shown, left.

A Christmas collage of country-French checks, prints, plaids, and even toile blends beautifully when ribbon-banded and tied together with grosgrain ribbon folded into prairie points.

A fresh wreath of greens, right, hangs over the Scandinavian-style daybed. White and red Christmas roses pay homage to the season, and playful spiral tops remind us of toys tots love to find in their stocking on Christmas morning.

For additional decorating inspiration with ribbon, please turn the page. You'll discover how Camela's peaceful porch retreat offers a friendly window to the world with a unique ribbon ornament framed against each tiny pane of glass. From left to right, choose from a galette, a double etoile with pinwheel center, or a cocarde. They're all made with geometric ribbons that create interesting patterns in their final festive form.

PEACEFUL RETREAT

A triple tier of rustic antiquity surprisingly complements the elegant moiré gift boxes, covered with ribbons and tassel trims. Ornaments made of treasured ribbons are waiting to be wrapped. One, on the far lower left, is made of an unusual French ribbon that's red satin on one side and iridescent green on the other. A bevy of pinwheel variations, étoiles, shooting stars, and galettes all can be combined and mixed and matched into unique one-of-a-kind tree trimmers.

For Camela, the promise of a perfect holiday season begins with the first day's delivery of dozens of season's greetings from friends and relatives both near and distant.

To display her favorites, Camela created a simple-but-stunning pocketed ribbon banner for Christmas cards that hangs on the weathered board wall of the porch, just inside the door for handy reference. A Christmas rose in bright red ribbon cleverly covers the unsightly nail.

WREATH

MATERIALS

- 18" Christmas wreath

- 1½ yards of 3"-wide striped grosgrain ribbon

- 3 yards of 1¾"-wide white wire-edge ribbon to make three Christmas roses (see page 92)

- 2 yards of 1¾"-wide red wire-edge ribbon to make two Christmas roses (see page 92)

- 2⅓ yards of 1½"-wide green wire-edge ribbon to make ten leaves (see page 104)

- 4 yards of 2"-wide Christmas ribbon to make one spiral top (see page 81)

- 4 yards of 2"-wide red polka dot ribbon to make one spiral top (see page 81)

- 1 yard each of 4"-wide Christmas ribbon and 3"-wide plaid ribbon

- Two tie-back cords; four 3" tassels

- Hot-glue gun and glue sticks

INSTRUCTIONS

1. Referring to the directions on page 31, create a serpentine edging from the striped ribbon. Glue the edging around the inside of the wreath.

2. Referring to the page indications in the materials list, make three white and two red roses, and two spiral tops. Create a flat bow with the 4" ribbon, and a four-loop bow with the plaid ribbon. Referring to the photo, glue the components in place.

SHADOWBOX

MATERIALS

- Supplies to make one Christmas flower (see page 90)

- 15½" x 12⅜" shadowbox frame (this one is 1⅝" deep with a 10" x 7½" opening)

- ½" yard of fabric of your choice

- A variety of matching ribbons and laces

- Three 8" pieces of ⅛"-wide green grosgrain ribbon

INSTRUCTIONS

1. Referring to the directions on pages 90–91, make one Christmas flower with two leaves.

2. Cover the base of the shadowbox with fabric. Cover the mat and the mat risers with fabric. Position the mat and risers in the box but do not secure yet. Place the flower on the base. Braid the green grosgrain ribbon. Place one end of the braid underneath the flower and one end underneath the bottom mat riser. When you are satisfied with the placement, glue the ends of the braid and the center back of the flower to the base.

3. Decorate the mat as desired with ribbons and lace.

STOCKINGS

MATERIALS

Note: The materials and instructions are for one green stocking. Other fabrics and similar ribbons may be substituted for a variety of results.

- **Stocking pattern on page 30, or pattern of your choice**
- **¾ yard of green moiré taffeta**
- **20" of 2"-wide reindeer jacquard ribbon**
- **18" of ⅞"-wide red satin ribbon**
- **20" of gold sew-in flat looped braid**
- **1 yard of 1½"-wide red grosgrain ribbon**
- **7" of ⅜"-wide flat gold trim**
- **Standard sewing supplies**

INSTRUCTIONS

1. Trace the reduced stocking pattern on page 30. Adjust the height of the stocking to 13½", the width at the top edge to 9", and the length of the foot to 12". Redraw the stocking shape and enlarge.

2. Using the pattern, cut out two stocking shapes from the taffeta, then reverse the pattern and cut out two more shapes.

3. Referring to the photo, left, baste gold looped braid 1½" below the top edge of one stocking shape. Place a length of reindeer ribbon across the shape, overlapping the bottom edge and basting line of the gold braid; topstitch in place.

4. Referring to the instructions on page 110, make about 16 single knife pleats in the red grosgrain ribbon, each about 1½" with a ½" to ¾" return. Slip the top edge of the pleated trim underneath the reindeer ribbon; topstitch in place.

5. Referring to the photo, baste gold looped braid at an angle from the top of the foot to the heel. Overlap the bottom edge of the braid with a length of red satin ribbon; topstitch in place. Overlap the satin ribbon with a length of reindeer ribbon; topstitch. Slip the edge of a length of red satin ribbon underneath the reindeer ribbon; topstitch in pace.

6. With right sides together and using ½" seam allowances, sew the decorated stocking and plain stocking shapes together. Sew the remaining shapes together for the lining, leaving a 4" opening in the center back seam.

7. With right sides together, slip the stocking into the lining stocking and stitch around the top edge, catching the ends of the flat gold trim in the seam allowance at the back seam for a hanging loop.

8. Pull the stocking out through the opening. Stitch the opening closed. Push the lining to the inside of the stocking; press.

QUILTED TABLE RUNNER

MATERIALS

- 17" x 67" piece of large-scale plaid fabric for the center of the table runner

- Four 12" squares of Toile de Jouy

- Two 4" x 67" pieces of small-scale plaid fabric for the borders and one 23" x 67" piece for the back of the table runner

- ¾ yard of green print for pieced stars and ends of table runner

- ½ yard of red print for pieced stars

- 4 yards of ½"-wide gold-edge striped grosgrain ribbon

- 6 yards of ⅜"-wide striped grosgrain ribbon

- 10 yards of 1"-wide green grosgrain ribbon to make the prairie-point edging (see pages 114–115)

- Low-loft quilt batting

- Matching threads

- Sewing machine; standard sewing supplies

INSTRUCTIONS

1. Referring to the illustration below, draw an equilateral triangle with 3½" sides onto paper. Add ¼" seam allowances to two of the sides; cut out. Using the star pattern, cut nine red and nine green print star segments.

2. Baste ½"-wide grosgrain ribbon to the edge of one-half of each star segment as shown below, mitering the point. Sew the star segments together in groups of three, alternating the colors as shown, then sew the halves together to complete each star. Make three stars.

3. Lay the four Toile de Jouy squares on point across the center of the large-scale plaid piece; center a pieced star on top wherever two squares meet.

4. Cut ⅜"-wide grosgrain ribbon to fit all the exposed edges of each square. Baste the ribbon in place, mitering the exposed corners and tucking the raw ends under the stars. Topstitch all the ribbons and stars in place.

5. With right sides together and ½" seam allowances, sew a small-scale plaid border to each long edge of the center plaid piece. Press.

6. Cut or tear a 24" square of green print fabric. Draw a large X through the center of the square, dividing it into four equal pieces, and cut on the drawn lines. With right sides together and ½" seam allowances, center and sew the 24" edge of one triangle to each end of the pieced runner. Center and sew the remaining two triangles to each end of the 23" x 67" piece of backing fabric. (The size of these triangles can be adjusted as desired to make a shorter or longer table runner.)

7. Use the pieced top as a pattern to cut the batting. Place the backing piece on the pieced top, right sides together, then lay the batting on top. Using a ½" seam allowance, stitch around the edges, leaving a large enough opening for turning. Turn the runner right side out; press. Turn in the raw edges at the opening and stitch closed.

8. Hand- or machine-quilt along the seams and, if desired, outline-quilt the shapes in the Toile the Jouy panels.

9. Referring to the instructions for making prairie points on pages 114–115, fold enough 1"-wide grosgrain ribbon to fit around the large-scale plaid. Stitch the prairie points in place; fold and press the points that face the center of the runner to the outside. Tack all points in place.

WINDOW ORNAMENTS

MATERIALS

- 3½ yards of 2"-wide Christmas ribbon to make one cocarde or galette (see pages 96–99)

- 5 yards of 1½"-wide Christmas ribbon to make two étoiles (see page 100) and two pinwheels (see page 106)

- 16" of 1"- to 1⅝"-wide organdy ribbon to make one M bow (see page 105)

- 3½" tassel for each cocarde or galette

- Cord for center of each pinwheel and for loop

- Standard sewing supplies

INSTRUCTIONS

1. Refer to the instructions on pages 96–97 to make a cocarde, or to the instructions on pages 98–99 to make a galette. Refer to the instructions on page 105 to make an M bow. Enhance the ornament with the M bow and tassel or as desired.

2. Cut sixteen 5" lengths of Christmas ribbon. Referring to the instructions on page 100, make two étoiles. Using the remainder of the Christmas ribbon, make two eight-pointed pinwheels. Sew the pinwheels to the centers of the étoiles. With the backs facing each other, sew the étoiles together in the center. Twist cord until it kinks into a knot; sew a knot to each pinwheel center.

FANCY BOXES

MATERIALS

- Purchased box or ¼"-thick balsa wood or foamcore board, metal ruler, and crafts knife

- Medium-weight moiré taffeta

- Several coordinating ribbons in a variety of widths including ⅜"-wide grosgrain

- 1 yard of 2"-wide gold-edge Christmas ribbon to make one pinwheel (see page 106)

- Fabric or crafts glue

- Purchased gold tassel

- Lightweight cardboard

- Scissors

INSTRUCTIONS

1. From balsa wood or foamcore board, cut two 3½" squares, two 2¼" x 3½" rectangles, and two 2¼" x 3" rectangles. Assemble the box as shown, right.

2. From lightweight cardboard, cut a piece to fit the outside bottom of the box, inside bottom of the box, and the inside of the lid. Center each cardboard piece on the wrong side of the moiré taffeta and cut a large enough piece of fabric to cover one side and the edges of each piece. Glue the cut edges of the fabric to the wrong side of each cardboard piece. Set aside.

3. Cover the outside of the box with a strip of moiré taffeta, gluing the top raw edges to the inside of the box and the bottom raw edges to the bottom of the box. Wrap ribbon around the outside of the box, creating your own design. Glue ribbons to the box so the ends rest against each other at a corner on the back of the box.

4. Place the lid on the box. Cut two 1½" lengths of ⅜" grosgrain for hinges. Turn ends turned under ¼" and glue half of each length, evenly spaced, to the top of the lid. Glue the remaining half to the back of the box. Cut and glue two more hinges to the inside of the box.

5. Line the sides on the inside of box either with a length of 3"-wide ribbon or a 3"-wide hemmed length of moiré taffeta. If preferred, cut extra-long pieces and gather to fit.

6. Glue the covered cardboard pieces to the inside of the lid, and to the inside and outside bottom of the box.

7. Referring to instructions on pages 106–107, create a pinwheel variation of your choice. Glue the pinwheel to the lid, catching the hanger of the tassel.

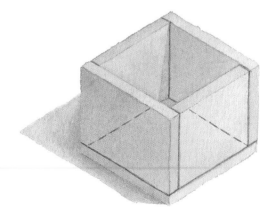

CARD HOLDER

MATERIALS

- Two 13½" x 26½" pieces and four 13½" x 6½" pieces of red moiré taffeta

- 2½ yards of ⅜"-wide striped grosgrain ribbon in holiday colors

- 1 yard of 1⅛"-wide ribbon with a holiday print

- 4 yards of ½"-wide antique gold lace edging

- 1 yard of ⅝"-wide antique gold flat lace

- 1 yard of antique gold cord for hanger

- Red and green thread

- One 4" red tassel

- 13½" length of ¼" dowel rod and two ¾" dowel caps painted metallic gold

- White chalk pencil

- Sewing machine; standard sewing supplies

INSTRUCTIONS

1. Fold one 13½" x 26½" piece of taffeta in half lengthwise and draw a curve along raw edges at bottom of folded piece. Cut the curve through both layers; open fabric. Use as a pattern to cut the back piece. Mark right side of front piece as shown, right.

2. For each pocket, sew two 13½" x 6½" pieces together along both 13½" edges, stitching with right sides together and ½" seam allowances. Make two pockets. Turn pockets right side out and press.

3. Pin a 13½" length of ⅝"-wide flat lace across the top of a pocket and lay a matching length of striped grosgrain across the bottom edge of the flat lace. Topstitch both lengths to the pocket in one step. Slip the top edge of a 13½" length of 1⅛"-wide ribbon under the bottom edge of the striped grosgrain and topstitch both to the pocket. Slip the top edge of a 13½" length of ½"-wide lace edging under the bottom edge of the 1⅛"-wide ribbon and topstitch both to pocket. Add ribbon and lace to second pocket in the same way.

4. Pin pockets to card holder between marked lines. Topstitch the bottom edges of three 13½" lengths of striped grosgrain to the top edges of three equal lengths of gold lace edging. Position the top edge of grosgrain along bottom edge of each pocket and topstitch ribbon and bottom of pockets to card holder in one step. Topstitch the remaining set to ribbon and lace line. On front of cardholder, baste lace edging to ½" seam line of side and bottom edges.

5. With right sides together and lace edging and pockets in between, sew two card holder pieces together along all but the top edge. Clip the curves, turn right side out, and press. Hand-sew a tassel to the bottom of the card holder.

6. Fold under 2" at the top and turn in raw edges ½". Topstitch closed, creating a casing for the dowel rod. Insert the dowel rod and glue a cap to each end. Tie the ends of the gold cord to the dowel rod.

FOLD LINE 2"

RIBBON AND LACE 1¼"

3½"

5½"

POCKET PLACEMENT

3"

5½"

POCKET PLACEMENT

5¾"

BON APPETIT

*G*ather 'round the table to
share fellowship, laughter, and
a bountiful harvest of holiday
joys. Atop an elegant linen
napkin, a petite ribbon posy
becomes the focus of a place
setting extraordinaire! Every
guest at the table finds a favor
to take home—lengths of
tubular ribbon filled
with gold and silver Jordan
almonds are tied at the ends
with gold-mesh bows. A
tassel-trimmed confection of
loops with a pinwheel center
graces each corner of the
fireplace mantel.

The essence of a holiday home is good food, good family and friends, and good cheer. Expressions of this sentiment puts every room of the house in a holiday mood, but it's in the dining room, when festive evenings are aglow with good wishes that gracious entertaining becomes the greatest joy.

Even the simplest fare takes on an air of elegance when accompanied by fancy trims and garnishes. A gift box dressed in gold foil wears an elegant wired organdy bow topped by an embellished pinwheel ornament.

The mantel, swagged with a simple roping and free from the usual hanging accoutrements, is decorated with fresh greens, fruit such as apples and kumquats, and twigs of holly, replete with clusters of bright red berries.

Pinecones, small and large cocardes, gold-mesh five-petal flowers, a tassel-trimmed galette, and more pinwheel ornaments embellish the face of a snow-tipped evergreen wreath. Lengths of knife-pleated silver ribbon fill out the composition and echo the glittering snow that covers the lawn in the background.

The lavish look spills over onto the dining table's stunning centerpiece: the Biedermeier— a *tour des fleurs* that's a labor of love well worth your time and effort, and certainly a family keepsake to grace the holiday table for years to come.

BON APPETIT

Christmas by candle- and firelight promises a most sensuous feast for the senses with a host of glorious ribbon accents for the window, tabletop, mantel, and more!

Perfectly proportioned and crowned with a light, feathery plume of M bows, the spectacular centerpiece, or Biedermeier, bursts with ribbon roses and flowers and adds color and drama when placed on an exquisite moiré table runner edged with ribbon and a pleated gold-ribbon petticoat flounce.

For Camela, it is a particular joy to create a variety of lavish ribbon embellishments to feature in the numerous get-togethers that ripple like golden harp notes throughout the busy holiday season.

BON APPETIT

In a home brimming with traditions, the holiday table gleams with antique silver and heirloom French pottery, crystal, and linens.

Presiding over the inviting scene and proudly claiming the center of attention stands the Biedermeier—a rich and glorious centerpiece of regimented rows of velvet roses, taffeta flowers, pods, and leaves, further enlivened with undulating waves of gathered gold-metallic and tubular taffeta ribbons. Waves of gold braid in the bottom row anchors the entire piece firmly in its setting.

The deep burgundy velvet and soft pink satin chou roses in the Biedermeier fit a perfect classic Christmas color scheme, but actually transcend the seasons when combined with the small blue five-petal flowers and light-color zinnias.

The pyramidal shape of the Biedermeier is one of Camela's favorites to create, and often in the summer she'll treat diners to a similar centerpiece made with fresh flowers on a chickenwire base. Whether you use freshly cut flowers from the garden or ones handcrafted from ribbon, make sure you pick a color scheme that highlights the season and the decorating scheme of your dining room for a stunning result that's a feast for the eyes!

PINWHEEL ORNAMENT

MATERIALS

- 27" of 1½"-wide burgundy striped velvet ribbon to make one pinwheel (see page 106)
- 4" of ⅝"-wide burgundy pleated ribbon
- 5" of 1/16" gold cording
- 8" of ½"-wide gold lace
- Standard sewing supplies

INSTRUCTIONS

1. Referring to the instructions on page 106, make one pinwheel.

2. Fold pleated ribbon in half, shiny side in; sew the ends together. Gather the bottom edge; fold ribbon flat with the shiny side out. Tie 5" of gold cording twice in the center; fold in half and pull the tails through the center of the gathered disc. Fringe the tails. Tack the disc to the center of the pinwheel.

3. Sew the ends of the gold lace together and gather into a wreath with a ¾" center opening. Slip the wreath over the disc. Attach the ends of the remaining cord to the inside of the top pinwheel point for a hanger.

MANTEL BOW

MATERIALS

- One complete pinwheel ornament (see top left)
- 1½ yards of 1½"-wide gold metallic ribbon
- 1¾ yards of 1½"-wide blue metallic ribbon
- 2 yards of 2"-wide red iridescent sheer ribbon
- Chair tie with 20" cord and 5" tassels
- Standard sewing supplies

INSTRUCTIONS

1. Referring to the instructions on page 105, make three large M bows—one gold bow with 5" loops and 12" tails, one blue bow with 5½" loops and 15" tails, and one red bow with 6" loops and 18" tails.

2. Tie a bow with the chair tie. Tack the three M bows and the chair-tie bow together.

3. Sew the pinwheel to the center of the bows.

WREATH

MATERIALS

- 18" pine wreath with pinecones

- Three pinwheel ornaments (see opposite)

- 1½ yards of 2"-wide gold mesh wire-edge ribbon to make two five-petal flowers (see page 102)

- Eight large red/yellow stamens

- 3½ yards of 1¾"-wide Christmas ribbon to make one cocarde (see page 96)

- 10" of 2"-wide red wire-edge ribbon to make one M bow (see page 105)

- 3½ yards of 1¾"-wide Christmas ribbon to make one galette (see page 98)

- 3 yards of 1½"-wide silver metallic ribbon to make three knife-pleat trims (see page 110)

- Two 4" gold tassels

- Standard sewing supplies

- Hot-glue gun and glue sticks

INSTRUCTIONS

1. Cut the gold-mesh ribbon in half. Referring to the instructions on page 102, make two gold-mesh five-petal flowers, each with 5" petals. Because the gold mesh frays very easily, begin sewing the petals 1" from the end. Bundle four stamens; fold the bundle in half. Sew the folded end to the center of the five-petal flower.

2. Referring to the instructions, opposite, make three pinwheel ornaments, complete with lace wreaths and gold-cord hangers.

3. Referring to the instructions on pages 96–99, make a cocarde and a galette. Make an M bow and attach it to the top of the cocarde. Tack a tassel to the bottom of each ornament.

4. Cut the silver metallic ribbon into three equal sections. Referring to the instructions on page 110, make three knife-pleated trims, each with 8, 9, or 10 pleats. Cut the ends of each trim piece in an inverted V shape.

5. Referring to the photo, top left, glue all the components in place.

Napkin Posy

Materials

- 15" of ⅝"-wide green wire-edge taffeta ribbon to make three leaves (see page 104)

- 30" of ⅝"-wide purple satin ribbon to make two chou roses (see page 94)

- 15" of ⅝"-wide rust satin ribbon to make one chou rose (see page 94)

- 17" of ⅝"-wide purple satin ribbon to make two five-petal flowers (see page 102)

- 8½" of ⅝"-wide rust satin ribbon to make one five-petal flower (see page 102)

- 24" of ⅝"-wide rust satin ribbon to make one zinnia (see page 123)

- 8" of ¼"-wide gold metallic antique braid

- 9" of ⅝"-wide green satin ribbon to make three wildflower pods (see page 121, and step 2, right)

- 4" of ⅝"-wide green pleated vintage satin ribbon

- 4" square of buckram

- 16" of ⅜"-wide green double velvet ribbon to make one M bow (see page 105)

- 12" of ¼"-wide gold metallic antique braid to make one M bow (see page 105)

- 4" square of felt; optional pin back

- Standard sewing supplies

Instructions

1. Referring to the instructions on the pages specified in the materials list, make three 2½" green leaves, two purple chou roses, one rust chou rose, two purple five-petal flowers, one rust five-petal flower, and one rust zinnia with fifteen 1½" petals. The five-petal flowers and the zinnia all have gold centers you make as follows: Cut the 8" piece of gold braid into four equal pieces; tie a knot in each piece. Before you tack the five-petal flowers to their buckram bases, push a gold knot in the center of each flower so the ends of the knot are on the back of the flower. Repeat in reverse with the zinnia so the ends of the knot are on the front of the zinnia; fray the ends.

2. When referring to page 121 to make the pods, add one more step: After the second edge has been drawn tight around the stuffing, secure the thread but do not clip. Bring the needle and thread up from the bottom and then back down through the pod several times, pulling the thread tight each time. Secure the thread and clip.

3. Gather one edge of the pleated vintage ribbon to 1½". Tack a ¼" pleat in the center of the gathered edge.

4. Lightly draw a 2½" x 2" oval shape on the buckram square. Referring to the photo, top left, arrange the flowers, pods, and pleated ribbon within the oval outline, overlapping each other slightly and grouping two of the three pods. When you are pleased with the arrangement, tack the components in place. Cut away excess buckram.

5. Sew the leaves to the back of the buckram. Make the M bows, then fold them in half so all the loops and tails are facing one way; tack to the back of the buckram. If desired, sew a pin back to the center of the felt oval. Sew the felt oval to the back of the posy so it can be worn as a pin.

TABLE RUNNER

MATERIALS

- 2 yards of 45"-wide off-white moiré taffeta
- 5 yards each of ⅜"-wide burgundy grosgrain ribbon and 1⅜"-wide blue-gold jacquard ribbon
- 12 yards of 1"-wide gold metallic ribbon
- Sewing machine; standard sewing supplies

INSTRUCTIONS

1. Cut two 65" x 18½" rectangles of moiré taffeta. With right sides together and ½" seam allowances, sew the two pieces togehter, leaving an opening for turning. Trim the corners and turn to the right side. Stitch the opening closed. Press the runner, especially the edges.

2. Referring to the instructions on page 110, press ¾" knife pleats in the gold metallic ribbon.

3. Overlap one edge of the knife-pleated ribbon with one edge of the jacquard ribbon and topstitch the two together. Place the overlapped and topstitched ribbon edge on the runner edge so the knife-pleated ribbon extends beyond the runner. Topstitch both edges of the jacquard ribbon to the runner, mitering the corners. Position the grosgrain ribbon next to the jacquard ribbon and topstitch in place, mitering the corners.

TABLE FAVOR

MATERIALS

- 8" of 4"-wide burgundy sheer tube ribbon
- 28" of ⅜"-wide gold metallic flat braid
- 6" of ⅛"-wide gold metallic flat braid
- Standard sewing supplies
- Candy

INSTRUCTIONS

1. Cut points in the ends of the tube ribbon. Sew a gathering line 1½" from each end. Gather the tube at one end; knot the thread. Fill the bag with candy. Gather and secure the other end of the tube.

2. Referring to the instructions on page 105, make two M bows from the ⅜"-wide gold braid. Using the ⅛"-wide braid, tie an M bow to each end of the favor.

BIEDERMEIER

MATERIALS

Note: The Biedermeier is built up of seven rows of flowers and six rows of gathered ribbon or braid. The materials list breaks down the materials needed for each row; however, some rows use the same ribbon, so before you shop for your supplies make sure you go through the list and add up all the same ribbons. Lengths of gathered antique gold flat lace were used to fill in between the flowers and to define the chou roses and zinnias.

- Sheet of foamcore board

- ¼ yard of green felt

- Masking tape; chalk pencil

- *Row 1:* 2 yards of ½"-wide gold flat braid

- *Row 2:* 6 yards of 1½"-wide blue iridescent rayon ribbon to make 24 five-petal flowers (see page 102)

- 1⅓ yards of thin gold cord to make 24 centers for the five-petal flowers (see page 103)

- *Row 3:* 9 yards of ⅞"-wide burgundy iridescent rayon ribbon to make 16 chou roses (see page 94)

- *Row 4:* 1½ yards of 1"-wide red-green iridescent tube ribbon

- 28" of ⅛"-wide gold metallic braid

- *Row 5:* 8 yards of ½"-wide antique gold ribbon to make 12 zinnias (see page 123)

- 48 stamens

- *Row 6:* 6 yards of 1"-wide burgundy velvet ribbon to make 12 chou roses (see page 94)

- *Row 7:* 1⅓ yards of ½"-wide gold flat braid

- *Row 8:* 6 yards of ⅞"-wide burgundy organdy-edge taffeta ribbon to make 12 five-petal flowers (see page 102)

- 48 stamens

- *Row 9:* 1⅓ yards of 1½"-wide blue-gray picot-edge ribbon to make 12 wildflower pods (see page 121)

- *Row 10:* ½ yard of 1"-wide antique gold lace with one scalloped edge

- *Row 11:* 24" of 1"-wide red-green iridescent tube ribbon

- 12" of ⅛"-wide gold metallic braid

- *Row 12:* 1 yard of 1"-wide antique gold lace with one scalloped edge

- *Row 13:* 2 yards of ⅞"-wide burgundy iridescent rayon ribbon to make four chou roses (see page 94)

- 6¼ yards of ⅝"-wide green wire-edge taffeta to make 44 leaves (see page 104)

- 3 yards of 1"-wide antique gold lace with one scalloped edge

- 1 yard of ½-wide gold flat braid to make loops

- 1 yard each of six different ribbons to make six M bows (see page 105)

- Standard sewing supplies

- Hot-glue gun and glue sticks

INSTRUCTIONS

1. Referring to the illustration, below, cut four triangles and one 8½" x 8½" base from foamcore board. Using the triangle and base pieces for patterns, cut four triangles and one base piece from green felt, adding a ½" margin all around the edges of each piece. Set the felt pieces aside.

2. Tape the four triangles together into a fan shape and, with the tape facing the inside, fold into a cone shape.

3. Place the base on a flat work surface. Set the cone shape over the base to make sure it will fit. If necessary, trim the edges of the base. Apply tape to all four outside seams, closing up the gaps and closing the fourth seam as well. Tape the base in place.

4. Glue the felt pieces in place, overlapping them at the sides and base to completely cover the structure.

5. To make sure that all the rows will be straight and even around the cone, and that you come out even when working from the bottom toward the top, make all the flowers first according to their instructions in the back of the book. Referring to the large photo on page 65 for placement, pin one flower of each row to one side of the cone, leaving enough space for the gathered ribbons and braids of Rows 1, 4, 7, 10, 11, and 12. Adjust their positions until you are sure that all rows will fit comfortably. Use a chalk pencil to lighty mark a placement line for each flower row around the cone.

6. Incorporating the ribbon-gathering steps below, begin attaching the rows to the cone, using small dots of hot glue to secure them in place.

7. Rows 1 and 7: Wrap thread around one end of the gold braid to prevent raveling. Get hold of two threads at the other end and carefully pull to gather the braid into a Serpentine. Place the braid around the cone and adjust the gathers until the ends meet. Wind the pulled thread around the end; secure with a knot.

8. Rows 4 and 11: Thread the iridescent tube ribbon onto the narrow gold braid. Place the ribbon around the cone; tack the ends of the narrow braid together.

9. Rows 10 and 12: Gather the straight edge of the gold lace to fit around the cone.

10. Cut forty-four 5" pieces of green taffeta; make 44 leaves. Randomly glue the leaves between the flowers. Cut 3" to 4" pieces of gold flat braid; fold in half and glue the ends between the flowers. Gather the remaining antique gold lace and weave in between and around the chou roses and zinnias for definition.

11. Bundle the M bows all together and pin or glue to the top of the Biedermeier.

GATHER TOGETHER

Radiant beams of light greet all who enter the living room, preparing guests and family alike for an evening filled with the holiday spirit. A host of heavenly ribbon ornaments entwined in the greenery surrounding the glorious gilded mirror casts a golden glow over the tradition-filled festivities.

Countless glass panes in the stately French doors reflect the glow of a thousand tiny lights emanating from the freshly cut tree, antique chandelier, and classic white candles. The holiday tree fills the living room with the glories of Christmas past and present. Trims and treasures lovingly collected over the years or received as gifts from friends and family share the branches with exquisite ribbon ornaments Camela loves to create whenever she has a moment to "play."

A delicate angel—arrayed in satin, seed pearls, and tiny ribbon pleats and braids—watches from the treetop over all the gilded splendor.

Each year, in anticipation of trimming the Christmas tree, Camela dreams up new and different ribbon ornaments to add to her growing collection of historic interpretations.

Three favorites are showcased on the opposite page, along with the cherished angel tree-topper.

Shown at upper left, the stunning étoile ornament features an overlay of metallic lace on a satin ribbon, echoing a similar treatment in the miniature star shapes once found in an antique shop—the shapes once decorated apparel, but adapted well as Christmas ornaments when joined into a garland, as shown here.

Shimmering in the glow of candlelight, the Bethlehem star, lower left, is fashioned in a manner similar to the étoile above it;

however, the center consists of a stuffing-filled tube, gently shaped into a star form. It's an adaptation of an old ornament made years ago for the millinery trade.

The spiral top featured lower right is a stunning confection of softly pleated organdy, trimmed with a profusion of M bows and a golden tassel.

The tree-top angel is a snap to make, thanks to the purchased porcelain head and hands. She sports wispy wings of sheer metallic striped ribbon folded into an open cocarde. The trim at the bottom of her glittering gold-embroidered dress consists of triple box-pleated ribbon with the top layers pinched together.

MIRROR ORNAMENTS

MATERIALS

- 2½ yards of ½"-wide gold metallic grosgrain ribbon for each shooting star ornament (see pages 116–119)

- 1½ yards of ⅝"-wide red metallic wire-edge ribbon for each small poinsettia ornament (see pages 112–113)

- 4 yellow stamens for each small poinsettia

- 26" of 1"-wide ribbon of your choice for each pinwheel ornament or pinwheel variation ornament (see pages 106–109)

- Gold cord for hanging

INSTRUCTIONS

1. Referring to the page numbers that are listed in the materials list, above, make as many ornaments as desired. Cut approximately 5"-long pieces of gold cord for hanging.

DOUBLE ÉTOILE TREE ORNAMENT

MATERIALS

- 4 yards each of ⅞"-wide cream-color double-face satin ribbon and ⅞"-wide antique-gold lace

- Two 3" squares of buckram

- 5"-length of gold cord

- Standard sewing supplies

INSTRUCTIONS

1. Cut twenty 5" lengths each of satin ribbon and antique-gold lace. Referring to the étoile instructions on page 100, sew five petals to the center of one buckram piece, layering the ribbon and lace and using them as one unit. Sew another five petals to the center, placing them between the first five petals. Sew the remaining ten petals to the second piece of buckram in similar fashion.

2. Cut the remaining ribbon and lace in half. Referring to steps 1–4 of the instructions for the cabochon rose on pages 88–89, make two rosebuds. After completing step 4, gather the remaining ribbon and lace and wind around the bud several times. Sew each rose to the center of an étoile. Trim each buckram piece into a circle.

3. Sew the circles together, cathing the ends of the cords in between the circles.

Spiral Top

Materials

- 4 yards of 3"-wide satin-edge cream organdy ribbon to make one spiral top ornament (see pages 96–99)
- ½ yard of 1½"-wide burgundy wire-edge ribbon
- ¾ yard of 2"-wide gold sheer ribbon
- 2 yards of 1½"-wide pink organdy ribbon
- ¾ yard of 1"-wide pink wire-edge taffeta ribbon to make one M bow (see page 105)
- 2" gold tassel
- 10" of gold cord for loop
- Standard sewing supplies

Instructions

1. Referring to the pages mentioned in the materials list above, make one spiral top and one M bow.

2. Cut the pink organdy ribbon in half. Tie two-loop bows from all remaining ribbons. Sew the M bows, two-loop bows, and ends of the cord to the top of the spiral top. Sew the tassel to the bottom.

Star of Bethlehem

Materials

- 2½ yards each of 1½"-wide gold metallic ribbon and gold metallic ricrac to make one étoile (see page 100)
- Two 2" squares of buckram; fiberfill
- 6" of gold cording for loop
- Sewing machine and standard sewing supplies

Instructions

1. Set aside 24"-lengths each of ribbon and ricrac. Sew the remaining ricrac onto the remaining gold ribbon with edges matching on one side; cut into twelve 5½" lengths. Referring to the étoile instructions on page 100 and the illustration, below right, sew six petals backwards to the center of the buckram; add another six face forward between the first six. Trim the buckram into a circle.

2. Sew the remaining ricrac onto the ribbon, ⅛" from the edge. Fold the ribbon lengthwise, rightside in, and sew the long edges together; turn right side out. Stuff tube with fiberfill; neatly sew ends together. Divide the tube into six even segments; sew across at each division. Bring the seams together, forming a star. Sew the star to the center of the étoile. Sew the ends of the cord to the edge of the buckram circle.

TREETOP ANGEL

MATERIALS

- Purchased head, hands, and wig
- ⅓ yard white bridal taffeta (body, dress lining)
- ⅓ yard embroidered and beaded gold metallic fabric (dress)
- 5" x 16" piece of gold lamé fabric (sleeve lining)
- 6" of 7"-wide white satin ribbon (body cover)
- 5" of 3"-wide white satin ribbon (arm cover)
- ½ yard of 2"-wide gold flat lace (sleeves)
- 5" of 1½"-wide gold metallic ribbon (armband)
- 5" of ⅜"-wide antique gold metallic ribbon (armband cuff)
- ½ yard of sew-in gold twisted braid (neck, halo)
- 1 yard of ¹⁄₁₆"-wide gold braid or cord (bodice and waist trim)
- 6 yards of 1"-wide gold metallic ribbon to make triple-box-pleated trim (see page 111)
- 2¼ yards of 2"-wide wire-edge gold ribbon to make a cocarde (see page 96)
- 7" x 7" piece of 7-count plastic canvas (body)
- Chenille stem; small amount of fiberfill
- One pair of pantyhose
- Fabric glue
- Sewing machine; standard sewing supplies

INSTRUCTIONS

1. Upper body: Cut a 4½" x 6" rectangle from white bridal taffeta. Fold the rectangle in half lengthwise, right sides together, and stitch with a ¼" seam allowance. Refold the tube so the seam is in the center instead of on the side. Stitch one end closed, curving slightly at the ends. Turn right side out; stuff with fiberfill. Turn in the raw bottom edges and neatly sew together.

2. Lower body: Roll the plastic canvas into a tube shape with a 1½" overlap—the tube should have a 1½" diameter.

3. Slip 1½" of the bottom of the upper body into the plastic canvas tube; hand-stitch to secure. Cover the tube with 7"-wide satin ribbon, neatly turning under the end that overlaps the starting end; hand-sew in place.

4. Arms: Insert the ends of the chenille stem into the hands. Measure and adjust the length of the chenille stem until the arms measure 11" from fingertip to fingertip; glue in place. Cutting around the circumference of the legs, cut a few long 1"-wide strips from the pantyhose. Glue the end of one strip to the top of one hand; tightly wrap the strip around the pipe cleaner to form arms. End by gluing to the opposite hand. Repeat until the arm is of proportionate thickness to the hand.

5. Position the arms across the top of the body and stitch in place. Position the head on top of the body; glue the head in place.

6. Cut the 3"-wide satin ribbon in half. Cover the upper arms with the ribbon, neatly turning under the end that overlaps the starting end; hand-sew in place. Repeat with the 1½"-wide gold metallic ribbon for the armband and the ⅜"-wide antique gold metallic ribbon for the cuff.

7. Dress: From the embroidered dress fabric, cut two 11" x 16½" rectangles for the body. Place the pieces together and fold in half so the 11" edges all meet. At the top corner of the piece measure 2" in across the top edge

and mark; measure 3¼" down along the side edges and mark. Connect the marks at each corner; cut to create armholes. From the taffeta lining fabric, cut two 10" x 10" squares for the body lining. Measure and cut armholes as you did for the dress body pieces.

8. Sleeves: Cut two 5" x 8" rectangles for the sleeves from dress fabric and two from lamé fabric. Stack the pieces. At the top corners of the stack measure 2" in across the top edge and mark; measure 3¼" down along the side edges and mark. Connect the marks at each corner; cut to create armholes.

9. With right sides together and ¼" seam allowances, sew the dress sleeves to the dress body front and back pieces at the armhole edges. Repeat for the lining sleeves and body pieces.

10. Sew the underarm and side seams in the dress and in the lining dress. Turn up and sew a ½" hem in each dress. Turn under the neck edge ¼" in each dress and sew a line of running stitches around each edge; do not cut the threads.

11. With wrong sides together, place the lining dress inside the dress. Pull the threads to gather each neck edge evenly—it should be almost as wide as the porcelain shoulder section. Knot the gathering threads. Tack the neck edges together. Beginning and ending at center back, hand-sew the sew-in edge of the twisted gold braid around the outside of the gathered neck edge—when finished, the twisted braid will roll over the sew-in edge.

12. Turn up and sew a ¼" hem in each sleeve; sew 2" gold flat lace to the hem of the dress sleeve.

13. Referring to the directions on page 11, make a triple-box-pleat trim with ½" pleats and sew to the bottom edge of the dress. Tack the top layers of each pleat together with a dab of fabric glue.

14. Slip the doll inside the dress through the dress' neck, guiding the arms through the sleeves as you lower her inside the dress. Glue the wig onto her head, arranging it so all the painted hair is covered. Sew the ends of a 5" length of twisted braid together for the halo. Fold the sew-in edge to the inside of the halo. Glue the halo onto the head.

15. Wrap the center of the ¹⁄₁₆"-wide cord snugly around the waist a few times, then bring the ends across the chest and cross over the shoulders a few times; knot in back. Arrange the dress pleats evenly at the waist.

16. Referring to the instructions on page 96, make a cocarde with 20 points but do not secure the first point to the last point. Tack the open cocarde to the back, just underneath the braided neck trim.

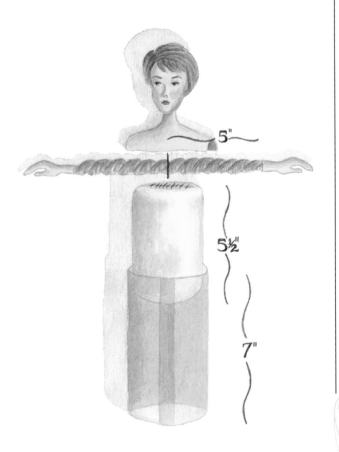

STEP-BY-STEP

*T*he following pages highlight specific
components that are necessary to
complete the projects featured at the end
of each preceding chapter. Some
components are inherent to their specific
projects, while other components, such as
the Poinsettia (pages 112–113), are
used in several projects, each requiring
its own set of measurements, amounts,
etc. A third type of component you'll
find in this section is a generic one—
this one can be used anytime, anywhere.
Please don't hesitate to substitute any of
the listed ribbons with ribbons of a
narrower width, different color, or
alternate weave or fabric. The fun is
in discovering each ribbon's effect on
its unique outcome!

BUTTON CENTER

MATERIALS

- 14" of 1"-wide gold metallic ribbon or a ribbon of your choice
- Standard sewing supplies

INSTRUCTIONS

1

1. Fold the ribbon in half; the right half will be called end A and the left half will be called end B. Fold end A back at the half point so that the V shape it creates is 60 degrees (an equilateral triangle).

2

2. Fold end A over the top of end B, as shown. Make sure the top edge of end A is flush with the fold at the half point and that all joints are accurate 60 degrees, as shown.

3

3. Bring end B up over end A and across the top, as before; the first of five equilateral triangles appears.

4. Keep folding ends A and B in this manner until all five equilateral triangles are completed. The selvedges meet neatly in the center. At this point it looks as if a sixth equilateral triangle is about to be completed; however, this partial triangle will be covered by the first triangle as described in the next step.

5. Bring end A, which is currently at the top of the fifth triangle, under the first triangle. Thread a needle with matching thread. Bring the first triangle up to complete the equilateral shape of the fifth, forming a slightly cupped shape. Stitch through all thicknesses from the outer corner where the first and fifth triangles meet to the center; secure the stitches and clip.

6. Trim ends A and B to about ½"; fold the ends underneath the cup. Sew a gathering thread about ½" to ¼" in from the outside edge of the cup. Pull up the thread tightly to form a button, tucking the excess gathers inside. Stitch closed firmly and clip. If you use a narrower ribbon for this center, e.g. ¾", work the gathering stitch closer to the edge.

SUGGESTED USE

Attach the button to the center of a double étoile: Make an étoile as instructed on page 100, then make a second étoile and sew the two together at the center, offsetting the points. Or, stitch a button to the center of a pinwheel; center the pinwheel on top of an étoile; tack to secure. Make two such units. Make a loop of gold cording and attach the ends of the cording to the center back of one unit, hiding the knot and stitches. Tack the units together, either with the star points matching or offsetting.

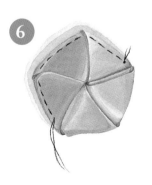

CABOCHON ROSE AND RENOIR ROSE

MATERIALS

- 1½ yards of 1½"-wide wire-edge taffeta ribbon in flower color of your choice

- 1 yard of 1½"-wide satin-edge sheer ribbon in flower color of your choice (for Renoir rose only)

- 3" square of buckram

- Standard sewing supplies

INSTRUCTIONS

1. Fold down 2" on the right-hand end of the taffeta ribbon as shown, so that 1" hangs down to form a "handle."

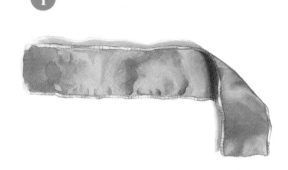

2. Fold the outermost half of the handle over onto the other half. This will become the center of the rose. Now roll the handle from right to left, coiling the ribbon loosely to make the rolled center of the rose.

3. When you have coiled two or three turns, and the top is a perfect circle, fold the top selvedge back to form a gentle bias fold, which will become the edge of a rose

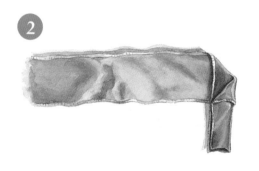

petal. Roll the rose to the left, so that the bias fold becomes part of the center. Hold the "handle" in your right hand as you roll; this will keep the rose loosely rolled. Secure the ribbon at the base of the rose with a few stitches.

4. Repeat this rolling and folding step once more, stitching to secure. Sew the center bud through the lower selvedge onto the buckram.

5. Find the end of the wire at the left-hand end of the lower selvedge. Push the ribbon down onto the wire, gathering the ribbon to about 11". Cut the protruding wire, leaving a short end. Bend the short end back and twist around the ribbon end. Securing the gathered ribbon from underneath, gently wind it around the bud in the same direction as you rolled the center, allowing a ¼" space between the gathered rows until it resembles a full-blown rose. When it is firmly attached to the buckram, trim the buckram close to the stitching.

6. A Renoir rose is basically the same as a cabochon rose; however, the Renoir rose has an additional length of ribbon coiled around the center bud for a softer, fuller effect. Work as follows: Follow steps 1–4 for the cabochon rose. Then, find the end of the wire at the left-hand end of the lower selvedge. Push the ribbon down onto the wire, gathering the ribbon to about 11". Cut the protruding wire, leaving a short end. Bend the short end back and twist around the ribbon end. Gather a 1-yard length of matching-color sheer ribbon to measure about 11". Secure one end of the sheer ribbon between the rosebud and the remaining gathered wire-edge ribbon.

Tacking down the gathered ribbons from underneath, gently wind them around the bud in the same direction as you rolled the center, allowing a ⅛" space between the gathered rows until it resembles a full-blown rose. When it is firmly attached to the buckram, trim the buckram close to the stitching.

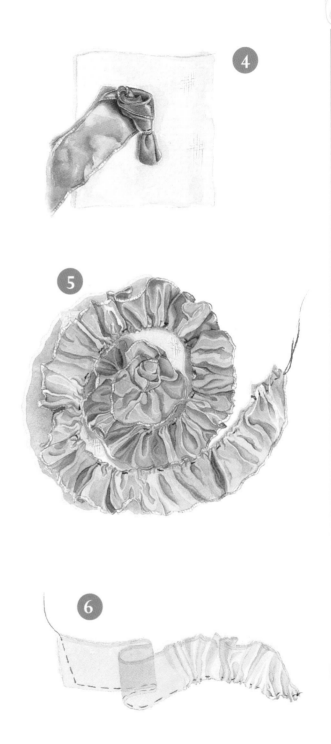

CHRISTMAS FLOWER

MATERIALS

- 1½ yards of 1"-wide red/white shaded wire-edge taffeta
- 3 yards of 1"-wide red wire-edge taffeta
- 17" of 1½"-wide green wire-edge taffeta for leaves
- 3" of ⅝"-wide yellow grosgrain
- 7" of ⅝"-wide yellow grosgrain
- 7" of ⅝"-wide brown grosgrain
- 3" square of buckram
- Standard sewing supplies

INSTRUCTIONS

1. Cut fifteen 7" pieces of red taffeta. Fold each piece in half widthwise. Cut nine 6" pieces of red/white shaded taffeta. Fold each piece in half widthwise, with the red shading at the top. Using small running stitches or machine straight stitches and beginning at the top of the cut end, sew diagonally to the folded end. Backstitch for ½"; knot and clip thread.

2. Trim the seam allowances ⅛" from the stitching lines; seal the cut edges with clear nail polish to prevent fraying.

3. Open each stitched ribbon into a petal.

4. Use a running stitch to join the red petals ¼" from the cut edges. Pull the thread tight to gather the petals. Connect the first petal to the last petal. Pull the thread tight to close the center of the flower; knot and clip the thread. Arrange the petals. Sew the flower to the buckram square.

Use a running stitch to join the nine red/white petals ¼" from the cut edges. Pull the thread tight to gather the petals. Connect the first petal to the last petal. Pull the thread tight to close the center of the flower; knot and clip the thread. Arrange the petals. Sew the center of the flower to the center of the red flower.

5. To make the center, cut the top selvedge from each piece of grosgrain. In each piece, make perpendicular cuts at 1" intervals to within ¼" of the lower selvedge. Be careful that you do not cut completely through the ribbon. Using a needle or awl, fray the ribbon to the ¼" level on all three pieces.

6. Place the short yellow strip on top of the brown strip and the brown strip on top of the long yellow strip, matching all left-hand edges. Beginning at the left end, roll up the strips, using brown thread to tack the selvedges together as you go. Position the rolled-up fringe in the center of the flower and tack to the flower and the buckram. Trim the buckram close to the stitching on the back of the flower.

7. For the leaves, cut one 10" and one 7" piece of green taffeta. Make two leaves according to the instructions on page 104.

1

CHRISTMAS ROSE

MATERIALS

- 29½" of 1½"-wide red metallic wire-edge ribbon or color of your choice
- 10" of 1½"-wide green wire-edge ribbon for large leaf
- 8" of 1½"-wide green wire-edge ribbon for medium leaf
- 3" square of buckram
- Stamens
- Standard sewing supplies

INSTRUCTIONS

1. Cut five 3½" pieces and four 3" pieces of red ribbon. Fold each piece in half widthwise.

2. With the fold at top, curl the top corners of one piece by rolling them onto a thin wooden skewer—you get a very neat and elegant curl with a wooden roller like the one shown. A plastic or metal knitting needle will do, but the ribbon rolls easier on wood.

3

3. Next, make a ¼" pleat in the center of the lower edge of the petal and secure with a couple of stitches. Make nine petals.

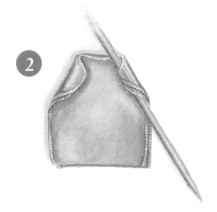

4. With the petals overlapping each other about a quarter of the width of each petal, use a running stitch to join the five large petals ¼" from the cut edges.

5. Connect the first petal to the last petal. Pull the thread tightly to almost close the center of the flower, leaving just enough room to poke the stamens through. Sew the center of the flower to the buckram square. Join the four smaller petals and place on top of the larger ones. (The Christmas flower is a variation on the seven-petal flower that was used for the illustration; however, the procedures are alike for either flower.)

6. Wrap the center of a small bundle of stamens with thread. Make a small hole in the buckram, through the center of the flower, and push the folded ends of the stamens through the hole to the backside of the buckram; secure to the buckram. Trim the buckram. Fluff out the stamens.

7. Referring to the instructions on page 104, make two leaves. Secure the end of each leaf to the buckram.

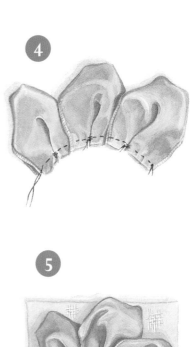

1

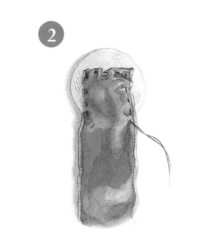

2

3

CHOU ROSE

MATERIALS

- 18" of 1"-wide velvet ribbon or ribbon of your choice
- 2" square of buckram
- Standard sewing supplies

INSTRUCTIONS

1. Cut a 1½"-diameter circle from the buckram, and carefully slash from the edge to the center. Overlap the cut edges about ¾" and stitch together along the edge, forming a cone shape.

2. Turn under ¼" at one end of the ribbon and place over the top of the cone. Using a knotted double thread, secure the ribbon to the buckram along the folded end and along the side edges with small running stitches. Let the needle and thread dangle in readiness for the next stitches.

3. Swing the ribbon counterclockwise a quarter turn, creating a diagonal fold on top of the cone. Stitch across the width of the ribbon from the lower right corner to the upper right corner.

4. Swing the ribbon counterclockwise another quarter turn, again creating a diagonal fold. Stitch across the width of the ribbon from the upper right corner to the upper left corner. Make a third quarter turn and stitch across the width again, gradually curving your line of stitches to follow the natural curve of the cone.

5. Make another quarter turn and secure the ribbon to the cone across the width. A small "window" should become visible in the center of the cone.

6. Position your subsequent folds just enough below the previous folds so the folds are not covered up—they form the petals of the rose. When the cone is completely covered with folds, trim the remaining length of ribbon and secure the end to the back of the buckram.

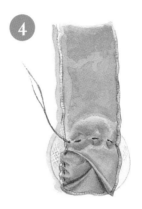

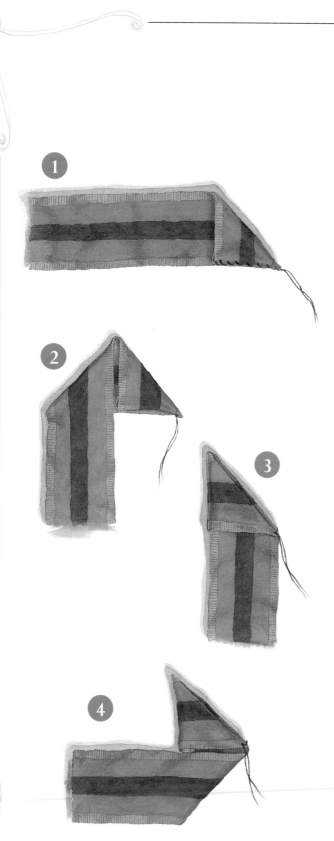

COCARDE

MATERIALS

- 50" of 1"-wide ribbon for a 25-point cocarde or
  2½ yards of 1½"-wide ribbon for a 30-point cocarde or
  3 yards and 21" of 2"-wide ribbon for a 32-point cocarde or
  4 yards and 26" of 2½"-wide ribbon for a 34-point cocarde

- Standard sewing supplies

INSTRUCTIONS

Note: The folding technique used to produce a cocarde is also the technique used to make the spiral top and the galette—both are shown on the next spread. A variety of ribbons can be used, from the narrow soft organdy ribbon used for the small cocarde ornaments in the music room, to the wider patterned grosgrain used for the ornaments in the porch window and on the porch wreath.

Practice with a few lengths of inexpensive, firm ribbon in a variety of widths. This will give you an idea of how the technique works and will also give you an indication of the yardage needed to complete a certain size cocarde. As a rule of thumb, figure the wider the ribbon, the more points you need, the longer your ribbon needs to be (see examples in materials list, above).

Our illustrations and instructions are for a 31-point cocarde, made with 2"-wide ribbon.

1. Turn under ½" of ribbon at one end. Turn the folded edge down so it rests on the bottom selvedge, forming a triangle. Using a knotted double thread, sew the edges together; knot the thread.

2. Fold the left end of the ribbon down so another triangle is created. At the center, leave about a ⅛" space so the selvedges from both the left and the right sides of the ribbon almost meet.

3. Fold the left triangle over the right triangle so the diagonal edges match. Secure the corner with a stitch and knot the thread, but do not cut it; let the needle and thread hang from the ribbon.

4. To form the next triangle, fold the length of ribbon upward to the bottom of the top triangle; leave a ⅛" gap, and crease the fold.

5. Fold the ribbon up, covering the top triangle.

6. Repeat Steps 3–5 until 31 points have been made. Turn under the final edge about ½" and secure with hidden stitches.

7. Pull up the thread firmly and backstitch about every two points. Join the first triangle to the last triangle to close the circle; this completes the cocarde. You can leave the points as they are or fold back every other one or every one for added variety.

8. If desired, continue with the instructions on the following pages to make a spiral top or galette.

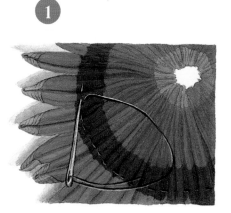

1

2

SPIRAL TOP
AND GALETTE

MATERIALS

- 46" of 1"-wide ribbon for a 23-point spiral top or galette or
  1 yard and 28" of 1"-wide ribbon for a 27-point spiral top or galette or
  2½ yards of 1½"-wide ribbon for a 32-point spiral top or galette or
  3 yards and 32" of 2"-wide ribbon for a 34-point spiral top or galette

- Standard sewing supplies

INSTRUCTIONS

Read the note and follow steps 1 through 7 of the cocarde instructions on pages 96–97, to make one complete cocarde.

1. Turn the cocarde over. The flat side is now facing up. Using double thread, sew running stitches through the center of the folds.

2. Pull up the thread until the ribbon forms a cup shape. Knot and cut the thread.

3. Sew running stitches through all the points that are sticking straight up. Pull thread up tightly until you have the same size center opening as on the reverse side. Knot and cut the thread. This completes the spiral top. Thread a double length of cord through the top and pull the ends of the cord through the loop. Attach a tassel to each end of the cord.

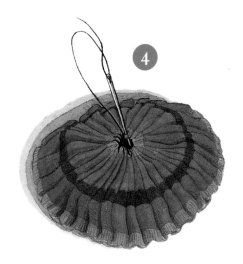

4. To make the galette, flatten the ribbon between your hands to form a doughnut or "galette" shape, pulling and pushing the folds until they lie down smoothly. Sew the edges of the center openings together.

5. Finish as desired.

ÉTOILE

MATERIALS

- 1⅔ yards each of 1"-wide blue double-face satin ribbon and 1"-wide silver metallic lace

- 10" of 1"-wide silver metallic lace for the ruffled center

- 6" of silver cording for a hanger

- One 3" buckram circle

- Standard sewing supplies

INSTRUCTIONS

1. Cut the ribbon and the lace each into twelve 5" pieces. Place a silver lace piece on top of a satin piece. With the lace side facing you, fold the right half of the unit over the left half. Secure with a stitch at the base of the crossed-over ends. Make twelve such points.

2. Attach seven points to the center of the buckram at equal distances.

3. Seven points complete the base of the étoile (the illustration shows a six-point variety). Place the remaining five points between the points that are already attached; secure with a few stitches.

4. Finish the étoile as desired. The one shown above features a pod with a ruffled center.

Twisted Étoile

Materials

- 2 yards of 1" wide gold metallic mesh ribbon
- 12" of 1" wide gold metallic lace for the ruffled center
- 6" of gold cording for a hanger
- One 3" buckram circle
- Standard sewing supplies

Instructions

1. Cut the ribbon into fourteen 5" pieces. Fold a piece in half; separate the halves.

2. Referring to the illustration, twist the right half counterclockwise.

3. Fold the right half over the left half. Secure with a stitch at the base of the crossed-over ends. Make fourteen such points.

4. Attach the finished points to the center of the buckram, overlapping them at equal distances.

5. Finish the twisted étoile as desired. The one shown above features a button center with a ruffle.

FIVE-PETAL FLOWER

MATERIALS

- 26" of 1⅛"-wide red plaid ribbon or 1⅜"-wide red/gold metallic ribbon or ribbon of your choice

- 2" square of buckram

- Standard sewing supplies

INSTRUCTIONS

Note: Shorter or longer lengths of ribbon may be used to make four-petal, five-petal, six-petal, or seven-petal flowers. Just make sure to divide the length of the ribbon, minus 1" for the seam allowances, by the desired amount of petals.

1. Starting ½" from one cut end of the ribbon, mark one selvedge at equal intervals. Beginning at the mark closest to one end and using double thread, take small stitches toward the opposite edge, then sew along the edge. Next, take small stitches toward the next mark; carry the last stitch around the selvedge. Continue to the end.

2. Pull the thread to gather the edge.

3. Join the first petal to the last; pull the thread tight. Knot the thread and and sew the flower to the buckram. Finish as desired.

Flower Center

Materials

- 2"-length of 2"-wide gold mesh or organdy ribbon in color of choice
- Small amount of polyester stuffing
- Standard sewing supplies
- Small seed or rocaille beads (optional)

Instructions

1. Cut as many 2" x 2" rectangles of gold metallic ribbon or organdy ribbon as desired. Allowing for a generous margin and using double thread, sew fairly large running stitches within the parameter of the rectangle.

2. Place a small amount of stuffing in the center of the rectangle. Pull up the threads to gather the ribbon fabric into a ball, enclosing the stuffing. Finish the flower center by winding the thread around the tail of the ball several times, forming a stem to help position the ball in the center of the flower.

3. If desired, flatten the ball and sew a few iridescent or gold beads on the surface for an added touch.

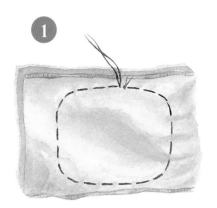

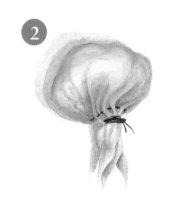

1

2

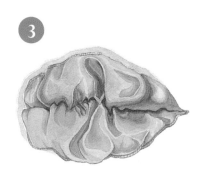

3

LEAF

MATERIALS

- Green wire-edge taffeta or ribbon of your choice
- Standard sewing supplies

INSTRUCTIONS

1. Cut the ribbon in as many pieces as instructed in the project's materials list. Fold each piece in half widthwise. Fold down the top corners, letting them rest just above the lower selvedge. Beginning at the bottom corner of the cut end, sew running stitches to the top selvedge, then along the top edge, then down to the opposite bottom corner.

2. Pull the thread until you obtain a pod-like shape. Back-stitch for about ½"; knot and clip the thread.

3. Open the layers. Adjust the gathers so the leaf is somewhat pear-shaped, with more gathers at the wide, bottom end and a smoother section at the narrow, tip end.

M Bow

Materials

- ½" to 2"-wide ribbon of your choice
- Standard sewing supplies

Instructions

1. Arrange a length of ribbon in an M shape. Using short running stitches, sew through the center of each of the four legs.

2. Gently pull up the gathering threads, forming a nice, soft bow.

3. If desired, edge your ribbon with a narrow lace or other decorative ribbon, tie the M bow in place with a matching or contrasting ribbon, or secure several bows at their centers for added fullness.

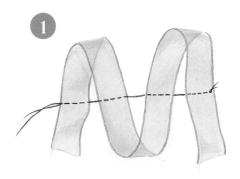

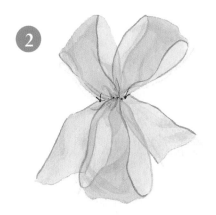

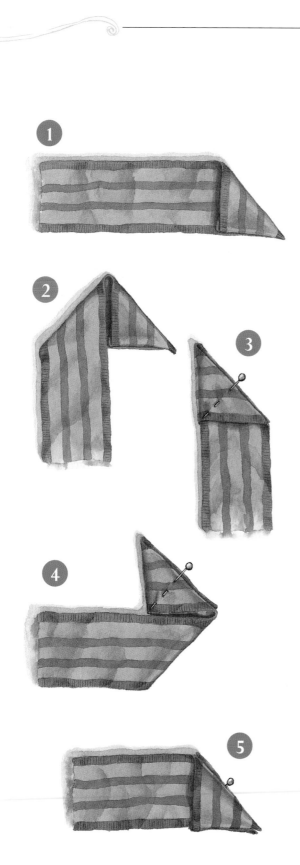

PINWHEEL

MATERIALS

- 27" of 1½"-wide burgundy striped-velvet ribbon or ribbon in length and width of your choice
- Standard sewing supplies

INSTRUCTIONS

1. Turn under the right-hand end about ¼" to create a finished edge. Fold this turned-under end of the ribbon down to the front and align the folded end with the bottom selvedge to form a triangle. Using knotted double thread, secure the bottom edge with hidden stitches; knot and clip the thread.

2. Fold the remaining length of the ribbon down and to the front so that another triangle shape is created. The selvedges will meet at the center, where you should leave about a ⅛" gap for folding room.

3. Fold the left triangle over the right triangle so the points match. Pin the center of the double triangle.

4. Fold the length of ribbon to the left, aligning the two selvedges in the center; leave a ⅛" gap and crease to create the next triangle.

5. Fold the bottom triangle over the top triangle so the points match.

6. Fold and crease the ribbon down. Fold the left triangle over the right triangle. Pin the center of the double triangle. You have just created 2 of the 7 points needed to complete the pinwheel shown, opposite.

7. Look closely at Fig. 7. Pivot the second point until it rests at an angle of 45 degrees (to the pin) or more to the first point. You can make the pinwheel as tight or loose as you wish by making the angle smaller or larger. Being careful not to include the first, bottom layer of ribbon, sew two backstitches through the three upper layers of the ribbon, at exactly the place shown in the illustration. Let the needle hang in readiness for the next stitches. If you stitch correctly, your stitches will be hidden, as each folded point will lie on top to hide them.

Fold up the ribbon length to the center, leaving a ⅛" gap, and crease to create the third triangle. Fold up the triangle to rest on the second triangle. Fold the ribbon length down and crease to create another triangle. Fold the left triangle over the right as shown to complete the third point. Pivot this third point 45 degrees to the right of the second point as before. The pinwheel shape will begin to appear. Stitch at the lower right side as before. Make the four remaining points in the same way.

8. To finish the pinwheel, trim the end of the ribbon to extend ½" beyond than the last triangle. Crease, and turn this edge under. Let it meet the selvedge and stitch, as in the beginning.

9. Bring the two ends together; slipstitch them together at the back. Rearrange the points at the desired angles, and whipstitch the center closed.

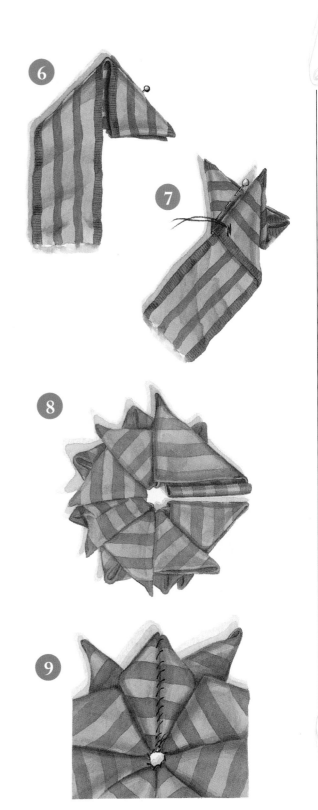

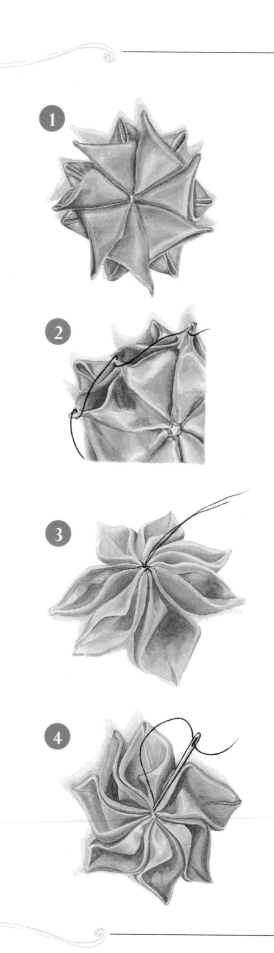

Pinwheel Variation

Instructions

1. Referring to the instructions and illustrations on pages 106–107 make a pinwheel with your choice of ribbon, adjusting the amount of points as desired.

2. Using a doubled thread, connect all the front points.

3. Pull the thread tightly so all the front points join in the center of the pinwheel.

4. Bring the needle from the front to the back of the center of the pinwheel, pulling the front points down into the center. Knot and clip the threads.

PINWHEEL VARIATIONS

INSTRUCTIONS

General: Referring to the instructions and illustrations on pages 106–107 make a pinwheel with your choice of wire-edge ribbon, adjusting the amount of points as desired.

1. Using a doubled thread, tack the center of the top edge of the front point to the center of the front point; repeat all around the pinwheel. Fold open the front points.

2. Turn back the tips of the front points. You can also turn back the tips of the points on the back of the étoile.

3. Using a doubled thread, tack the center of the top edge of the front point to the center of the pinwheel; repeat all around the pinwheel. Fold open the front points.

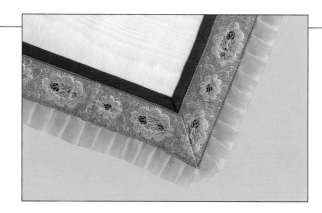

PLEAT–SINGLE KNIFE

MATERIALS

- Ribbon of your choice
- Cardboard
- Standard sewing supplies

INSTRUCTIONS

To make single knife pleats in any width ribbon, multiply the depth of the pleat by 3.5, then multiply the resulting number by the desired length of the pleated ribbon. Example: For a 24" length of trim with 1" knife pleats you will need (1" x 3.5) x 24" = 84". (Add an additional ½" at each end for turning under.) For a less regimented effect, reduce the depth of the pleat. The pleats can be formed as you go; however, it's best to use gauges when beginning.

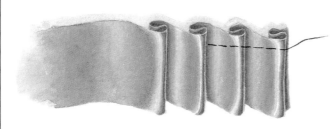

1. Cut two 1" x 3" cardboard gauges. Place one gauge across the ribbon, ½" from one end. Fold the long end over the gauge and crease the fold (Fold 1). Place the second gauge on the ribbon, directly over the first. Fold the long end over the gauge again and crease the fold (Fold 2)—one pleat made. Remove the gauges. Use a double thread to secure each pleat as you go.

2. To form the next pleat, place a gauge across the ribbon about ¼" to ½" from Fold 2. Fold the ribbon over the gauge; crease. Place the second gauge on the ribbon, directly over the first. Fold the ribbon over the gauge again and crease. Remove the gauges and tack the pleat in place, letting the needle hang free in back. Continue in this manner to the end of the ribbon.

PLEAT–TRIPLE-BOX

MATERIALS

- Ribbon of your choice
- ¼"-wide ribbon (optional)
- Cardboard
- Standard sewing supplies

INSTRUCTIONS

A triple box pleat consists of six pleats; three pleats facing one direction and three pleats facing the opposite direction. To calculate the length of ribbon needed, use the following formula: (depth of pleat x 5.5) x desired length. Example: For a 24" length of trim with 1½" pleats you will need (5.5 x 1.5") x 24" = 198" or 5½ yards. (Add an additional ½" at each end for turning under.)

1. Using ½" x 3" gauges, make one knife pleat as directed in the pleating instructions, opposite. Repeat the instructions two more times in the same spot on the ribbon, completing one half of a triple box pleat.

2. Turn the ribbon over and make another set of three knife pleats, completing the second half of the triple box pleat. Tack the two sets of pleats together in the center, turn the ribbon over, and continue the process to the end of the ribbon.

3. If desired, tack the centers of the top pleats to each other and run a decorative ribbon through the created center openings.

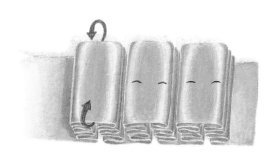

1

2

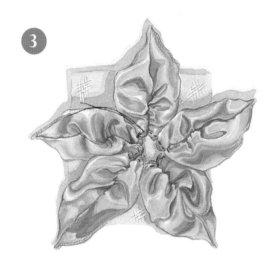

3

POINSETTIA

MATERIALS

One large poinsettia:
- 2½ yards of 1¾"-wide red metallic wire-edge ribbon

- 63" of ½"-wide gold metallic braid

- One large yellow stamen

- Eight yellow/red stamens

- 4" square each of buckram and felt

- Standard sewing supplies

One medium poinsettia:
- 2 yards of 1½"-wide red metallic wire-edge ribbon

- Four yellow/red stamens

- 3" square each of buckram and felt for medium poinsettia

- Standard sewing supplies

One small poinsettia:
- 1⅓ yards of ⅝"-wide red metallic wire-edge ribbon

- Four yellow/red stamens

- 2" square each of buckram and felt

- Standard sewing supplies

INSTRUCTIONS

1. Depending on the desired size, cut the 2½-yard ribbon into nine 10" pieces, cut the 2-yard ribbon into nine 8" pieces, or cut the 1⅓-yard ribbon into eight 6" pieces. Fold each piece in half widthwise. Fold down the top corners, letting them rest just above the lower selvedge. Beginning at the bottom corner of the cut end, sew running stitches to the top selvedge, then along the top edge, then down to the opposite bottom corner.

2. Pull the thread until you obtain a pod-like shape. Backstitch for about ½"; knot and clip the thread. Open the layers. Adjust the gathers so the leaves are somewhat pear-shaped, with more gathers at the wide, bottom end and a smoother section at the narrow, tip end.

3. For all sizes, use a running stitch to join five leaves ¼" from the cut edges. Connect the first petal to the last petal. Pull the thread tightly to almost close the center, leaving just enough room to poke the stamens through. Sew the center of the flower to the buckram square.

4. Join the four or three remaining leaves and secure on top of the larger ones. Wrap the center of the stamens with thread.

5. For the large poinsettia, tie an overhand knot about 3½" from each end of the gold braid. Tie an overhand knot every 7" between the end knots. Referring to the illustration, right, fold the ribbon so the knots are all at one end, and the ribbon tails and the folds on the other end. Secure the tails and folds with a few stitches, catching the bundle of stamens at the same time. Poke a hole through the buckram in the center of the flower to push stamens and gold braid through towards back; secure to the buckram. Trim the buckram to a circle; cover with felt.

6. Make a small hole in the buckram, through the center of the flower, and push the folded ends of the stamens through the hole to the backside of the buckram; secure to the buckram. Trim the buckram to a circle; cover with felt. Fluff the stamens.

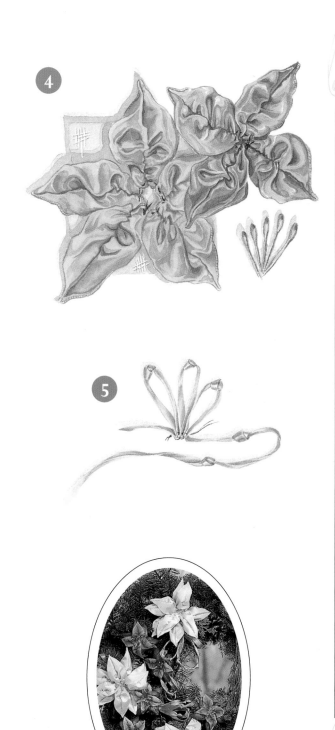

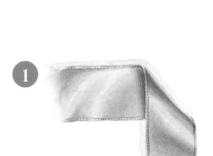

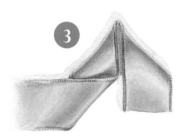

Prairie Points

Materials

- 10 yards of 1"-wide green grosgrain ribbon (or plan twice the amount of ribbon for the finished amount of prairie points)

- Fabric glue (optional)

Instructions

1. Turn down the right-hand end of the grosgrain ribbon so it extends ½" beyond the bottom selvedge, forming a triangle.

2. Fold down the left end of the ribbon so another triangle is created. At the center, leave about a ⅛" space so the selvedges from both the left and the right sides of the ribbon almost meet; press. This completes the first open prairie point, so called because it has a center opening.

3. Fold the left end of the ribbon to the left so it is horizontally positioned; press.

4. To form the next triangle, fold the length of ribbon away from you and upward at a right angle. This completes the first closed prairie point, so called because it has no center opening.

5. Fold the length of ribbon toward you and to the left.

6. Fold down the left end of the ribbon so another triangle is created. At the center, leave about a ⅛" space so the selvedges from both the left and the right sides of the ribbon almost meet; press. This completes the second open prairie point.

If your triangles do not hold their shape, apply a tiny dab of fabric glue between the layers of each triangle.

Continue folding until the desired length of your trim is completed.

7. Position the prairie-point trim on your project; topstitch horizontally through the center of the points along seam line between the large-scale and small-scale plaids. Press the open points down, creating all closed points. If desired, hand tack the tip of each prairie point to the base fabric so they don't jump up.

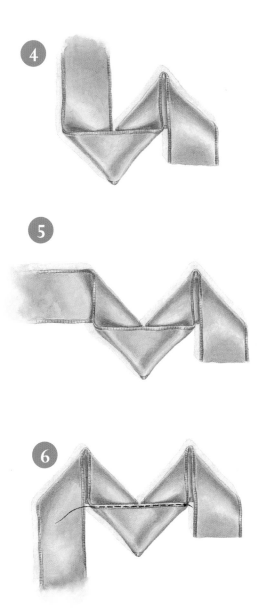

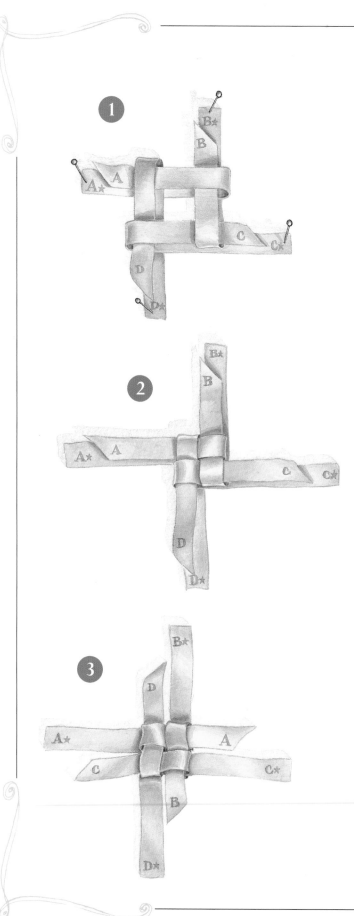

SHOOTING STAR

MATERIALS

- Four 22"-long and ½"-wide gold metallic grosgrain ribbons

- 10" of gold cord for hanger

- Foamcore board and pins

INSTRUCTIONS

1. Lay out the ribbons exactly as shown in Fig. 1 and pin to a foamcore board to hold them in place as you work. Mark the ends exactly as shown to help you follow the diagrams. The first side of the star will be made using ends A, B, C, and D, and the reverse will use the ends marked with the letters plus *.

2. Begin with the basketweave as shown in Fig. 1, then tighten the ribbons and, if desired, pin the ends as shown in Fig. 1.

3. Make a second basketweave: bring A to the right, fold B down and over A, fold C to the left and over B, then fold D up and thread it under the loop created by A. Finish this step by threading D through the loop created in A. Draw the 4 ribbon ends tight, and repin to secure.

4. Take A and twist it counterclockwise and upward so it lies alongside B*. Crease the fold firmly. Repeat in pinwheel fashion with B, C, and D.

5. Take A and make a second fold so it lays parallel with and on top of D; crease the fold.

6. Flip A down toward you so it lays parallel with and on top of A*. Thread A through the loop made by B. You should have a small double triangle.

continued on page 118

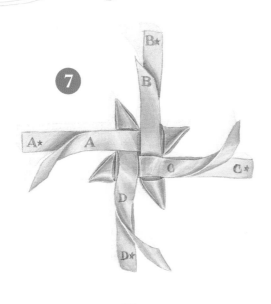

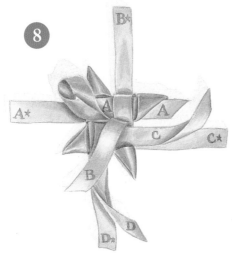

continued from page 117

SHOOTING STAR

7. Working clockwise, repeat Step 6 with B, C, and D. When all four are completed, all ribbons should be positioned in letter-matching pairs.

8. This is where the four loops are created: Fold B down and out of the way. Take A and twist it in a clockwise motion away from you and then back down again, coiling it exactly as shown. Slide the end A under the B loop, and push it through the center of the double triangle made by A. Draw A tight to create a firm loop.

9. Repeat Step 8 with B, C, and D. Draw the ribbons tight to create firm loops.

10. Now make the other, identical side of the shooting star: Take out the holding pins, carefully turn the whole star over, and pin to the board. Reveal the original basketweave by pulling back the long ends (the *). Make another basketweave with these long ends A*, B*, C*, and D* to secure this side, as described in #3 (Fig 3) page 116. Then it will resemble Fig. 10.

11. Repeat step 4 with these new ends as shown in Fig. 11, which shows the exact location of each end when first creases are made.

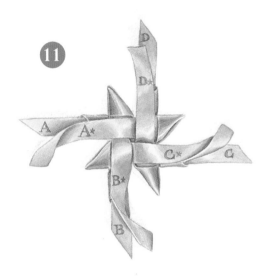

12. Fold and crease again, and thread through the loops as before, creating four new points. Now create the four top curls as before, see Fig. 8, opposite. When finished, take out the pins, draw the ribbons tight, and trim the ends.

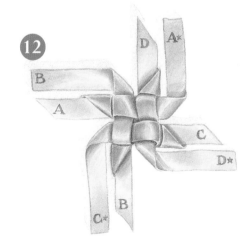

1

2

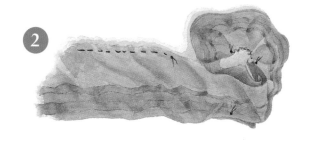

Turbine Rose

Materials

- 3 yards of 3"-wide cut-velvet ribbon or ribbon of your choice
- Standard sewing supplies

Instructions

1. Measure and mark one selvedge of the ribbon as follows: ½" seam allowance at one end, then 3" space, 8" space, 3" space, 8" space, etc., until you have nine 8" spaces. End with a 3" space and ½" seam allowance. Cut off the remaining ribbon. Measure and mark the halfway point of each 3" space on the opposite selvedge.

2. Using doubled thread, tightly gather the 8" sections, securing the thread with a knot after each section. Coil the first section on itself and tack the first two halfway points together. The tacked halfway points will form the center of the rose.

3

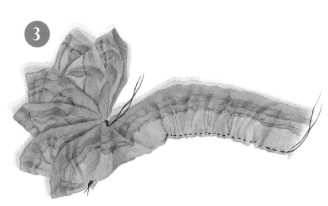

3. Continue to coil the gathered ribbon in a clockwise motion, sewing with double thread through the halfway points. Finish the rose as instructed on page 26.

WILDFLOWER POD

MATERIALS

- 1"-wide ribbon of your choice
- Standard sewing supplies

INSTRUCTIONS

1. Cut a 4" piece of ribbon. Fold the ribbon piece in half widthwise and sew a seam ¼" from the cut ends. Turn the seam to the inside.

2. Sew running stitches around the perimeter, ¼" below the top selvedge.

3. Pull the thread tightly to gather; knot thread. Place a small amount of stuffing inside. Sew running stitches closely around bottom selvedge.

4. Pull the thread tightly to gather; knot thread.

WOVEN RIBBONS

SELECTING RIBBONS

Choosing ribbons of the same shade or closely related shades of one color is fairly easy—three to five textures and widths of ribbon make a lovely pattern. There are no hard and fast rules. To make your first weaving project easier, choose all ribbons of 1" width. If you feel adventurous, select ribbons of varying widths, say ½" to 1½". Weaving is a wonderfully creative way to use up leftover ribbon—if you have long lengths you can make a sizeable pillow top, and with short lengths you can make a purse or mini pillow. To cover a large item with woven-ribbon fabric, draw ribbon-simulating guidelines on your pattern with a variety of widths between the lines. Measure the lengths of the pretend ribbons, then double the amounts to make sure you have enough ribbon to weave in the other direction.

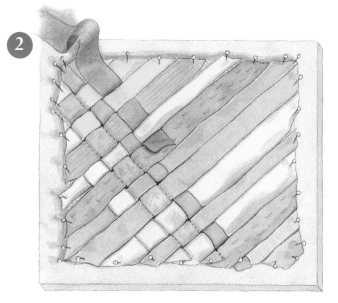

WEAVING THE RIBBONS

1. With the adhesive side up, secure the corners of the iron-on interfacing with pins to a foamcore board. Place the first ribbon at an angle on the interfacing and pin at the beginning and the end. Continue laying out ribbons above and below the first ribbon, pinning as you go and keeping them closely aligned and parallel, to cover the entire piece of interfacing.

2. Starting in one corner, weave a long ribbon through the completed first layer and secure the ends with pins. Then continue weaving ribbons above and below this ribbon, making sure the ribbons align, leaving no gaps.

3. With your iron on the steam setting and a damp cloth over the woven-ribbon fabric, press the iron on the fabric in an up and down motion, fusing the ribbons to the interfacing. Fold back the pressing cloth and remove the pins from one edge only; replace the cloth and press that edge. Repeat with the other edges. Turn the woven-ribbon fabric over and carefully press the back. Making sure your desired pattern includes a generous seam allowance, place the pattern on the woven-ribbon fabric and lightly draw around it. Stitch on the drawn pattern line(s). Trim away the excess ribbon ends.

ZINNIA

MATERIALS

- 23½" of ⅝"-wide ruched iridescent ribbon
- Stamens
- 2" square of buckram

INSTRUCTIONS

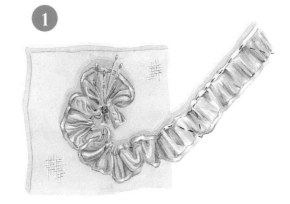

1. Starting ½" from one cut end of the ribbon, mark one selvedge at 1½" intervals. Beginning at the mark closest to one end and using double thread, take small stitches toward the opposite edge, then sew along the edge. Next, take small stitches toward the next mark; carry the last stitch around the selvedge. Continue to the end. Pull the thread tight, gathering the ribbon to an 11" length; knot the thread.

Gather a bunch of stamens. Fold the bunch in half and wrap it with thread or stem wire. Place the stamens at the end of the gathered ribbon and secure it to the center of the buckram square.

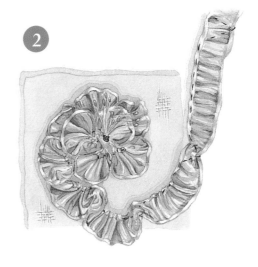

2. Coil three of the petal-shape gathers around the stamens. Secure in place; then secure to the center of the buckram. Coil the remaining ribbon around the center, tacking the selvedges of the inner petals to the buckram as you go. Trim the buckram close to the stitching in back.

SOURCES

ARTEMIS
179 High St.
South Portland, ME 04106
(207) 741-2509, Fax (207) 741-2497
Hand-dyed bias silk ribbons
Distributor of Hanah Silk
Retail and wholesale

BELL'OCCHIO
8 Brady St.
San Francisco, CA 94103
(415) 864-4048, Fax (415) 864-2626
New and vintage ribbons, millinery flowers
Retail

BRIMAR, INC.
1500 Old Deerfield Rd., Suite 5
Highland Park, IL 60035
(847) 831-2120, Fax (847) 831-3531
Tassels, cording, braids, metallic ribbons
Retail, wholesale; catalog available

BRITEX
146 Geary St.
San Francisco, CA 94108
(415) 392-2910, Fax (415) 392-3906
Fabric, ribbons, buttons, trims, buckram
Retail

CAMELA NITSCHKE RIBBONRY
119 Louisiana Ave.
Perrysburg, OH 43551
(419) 872-0073, Fax (419) 872-0073
Web address: http://www.ribbonry.com
Imported ribbons, wired ribbons, Mokuba
ribbons, books, videos, kits, buckram, stamens
Retail, wholesale; mail-order available

CATAN FLORAL
17647 Foltz Ind. Pkwy.
Strongsville, OH 44136
(800) 321-1494, Fax (216) 572-9954
Large crafts supply store
Retail, no mail-order

CREATIVE IMPORT
10 Belgrade Ave.
Youngstown, OH 44505
(330) 759-1554
Ribbons
Wholesale

ELSIE'S EXQUISIQUES
P.O. Box 7177
Laguna Niguel, CA 92607
(714) 831-3781, Fax (714) 831-3390
Orders only: (800) 742-SILK
Ribbons, trims, miniature flowers,
stamens, silk, miniature grosgrain
Retail, wholesale; catalog available

FINNS FABRICS BY DYLLIS
113 N. Cook St.
Barrington, IL 60010
(847) 381-5020
Fabric
Retail

GRAYBLOCK
P.O. Box 967
28370 St. Michael's Rd.
Easton, MD 21601
Fax (410) 820-6048
Ribbons
Wholesale

HYMAN HENDLER
67 W. 38th St.
New York, NY 10018
(212) 840-8393
French jacquard and wired ribbons, trims, tassels
Retail, wholesale

LACIS
3163 Adeline Ave.
Berkeley, CA 94703
(510) 843-7178, Fax (510) 843-5018
Lace supplies, ribbons, tassels, stamens, beads
Retail, wholesale; catalog available

LES TISSUS COLBERT
The Foundry
712 W. Northwest Hwy.
Barrington, IL 60010
(847) 382-6076
Fabric
Retail

M & J TRIMMING COMPANY
1008 and 1014 6th Ave.
New York, NY 10018
(212) 391-9072
Trims, braids, ribbons, beaded appliqués, fringes
Retail, wholesale

MKB
561 7th Ave. 11th Floor
New York, NY 10018
(212) 302-5010
Web address: http://www.festivegiftwrap.com
Mokuba ribbons, call for distributors
Wholesale

MIDORI, INC.
3524 W. Government Way
Seattle, WA 98119
(206) 282-3595
Ribbons
Wholesale

NANCY'S SEWING BASKET
2221 Queen Anne Ave. North
Seattle, WA 98109
(206) 282-9112, Fax (206) 282-7321
Fabric, supplies, ribbon
Retail

RUBAN ET FLEUR
8655 Sepulveda Blvd.
Westchester, CA 90045
(310) 641-3466, Fax (310) 641-1211
Wired ribbon, stamens, jacquard ribbon, buckram
Retail, wholesale; catalog available

SO GOOD
28 W. 38th St.
New York, NY 10018
(212) 398-9236, Fax (212) 768-1325
Ribbons
Wholesale

TALLINA'S
15791 SE Highway 224
Clackamas, OR 97015
(503) 658-6148
Retail, wholesale; catalog available

TINSEL TRADING COMPANY
47 West 38th St.
New York, NY 10018
(212) 730-1030, Fax (212) 768-8823
Antique trims, braids, ribbons, trims,
1900s metallic trims
Retail, wholesale; video, catalog available

VABAN-GILLE, INC.
P.O. Box 420747
San Francisco, CA 94142
(415) 552-5490
Ribbons
Wholesale

YLI CORPORATION
PO Box 420-747
San Francisco, CA 94142
Fax (415) 255-2329
Pure silk ribbon, thread, yarn
Retail, wholesale; catalog available

INDEX

This book is dedicated to my mother and
first teacher, Jane Hess.
I would like to thank all of the members of my
family, especially my husband Steve, for
their continuing support.

Many thanks once again to my staff at The Ribbonry
for all their hard work: Alice Croy,
Marguerite Nagy, Jan Niles, Natalie Tallon,
Marge Tiefenbach, and Gloria Weller.

I want to express my deepest appreciation to
Hyman Hendler in New York for being an early source
in my search for beautiful French ribbons.

A special acknowledgement to Marge Tiefenbach
for allowing me to use her doll and dress
pattern for the gold angel.

Thank you also to Liz Barry, Lynn Buri,
and Hazel Hayden.

Camela

SELECT PUBLICATIONS FROM MARTINGALE & COMPANY

HOLIDAY QUILTS AND CRAFTS

Appliquilt® for Christmas • Tonee White
Coxcomb Quilt • Donna Hanson Eines
Easy Seasonal Wall Quilts • Deborah J. Moffett-Hall
Folded Fabric Fun • Nancy J. Martin
Quick-Sew Celebrations
Quilted for Christmas
Quilted for Christmas, Book II
Quilted for Christmas, Book III
Quilted for Christmas, Book IV
Welcome to the North Pole • Piece O' Cake
   Designs, Inc.

HOME DECORATING

Decorate with Quilts & Collections
   • Nancy J. Martin
The Home Decorator's Stamping Book
   • Linda Barker
Living with Little Quilts • Alice Berg,
   Mary Ellen Von Holt & Sylvia Johnson
Make Room for Quilts • Nancy J. Martin
Soft Furnishings for Your Home
   • Sharyn Skrabanich
Welcome Home™: Debbie Mumm

STITCHERY/NEEDLE ARTS

Baltimore Bouquets • Mimi Dietrich
Crazy but Piecable • Hollie A. Milne
Hand-Stitched Samplers from I Done My Best
   • Saundra White
Machine Needlelace • Judy Simmons
Miniature Baltimore Album Quilts
   • Jenifer Buechel
A Passion for Ribbonry • Camela Nitschke
A Silk-Ribbon Album • Jenifer Buechel
Victorian Elegance • Lezette Thomason

WEARABLES

Crazy Rags • Deborah Brunner
Dress Daze • Judy Murrah
Dressed by the Best
Easy Reversible Vests • Carol Doak
Jacket Jazz • Judy Murrah
Jacket Jazz Encore • Judy Murrah
More Jazz from Judy Murrah
Quick-Sew Fleece
Sew a Work of Art Inside and Out
   • Charlotte Bird
Variations in Chenille • Nanette Holmberg

Many of these books are available at your local fabric, quilt, or craft shop.
For more information, call, write, fax, or email for a free color catalog.

Martingale & Company
PO Box 118
Bothell, WA 98041-0118 USA

Toll-free: 1-800-426-3126
Int'l: 425-483-3313
24-Hour Fax: 425-486-7596
E-mail: info@patchwork.com
Web: www.patchwork.com